P9-AOT-549

Religious Values in Education

Religious Values in Education

BY

WARD MADDEN
Assistant Professor of Education
Brooklyn College, New York

Harper & Brothers Publishers
New York

RELIGIOUS VALUES IN EDUCATION

Printed in the United States of America

FIRST EDITION

H-A

To

Vern Sayers and George Axtelle

in appreciation and gratitude

Contents

Preface

My purpose in writing this book is to suggest how education can in its normal and natural course help in building a spiritual outlook adequate to the needs of the young people of our age. The state in which the modern mind finds itself emphasizes the importance of such an undertaking. For some time I have been sounding out the attitudes toward religion of my own students in upper-division and graduate classes of this large, metropolitan college. A few, not more than 10 per cent, feel they can find spiritual fulfillment in the traditional supernatural forms of religion. Another group, no larger than the first, is at the opposite end of the scale. The members of this latter group are essentially antagonistic to religion, and they substitute for it an ethical approach to life founded on a naturalistic world view.

Gravitating between these two poles, attracted by both but unable to come to rest with their less numerous fellows at either, are the great majority of students. They are confused, dissatisfied, and groping. I believe these students are representative of the mentality of our age. They are the older, more mature students in this public college, located in one of the great centers of Western culture. They have grown up in a society oriented to the Judaic-Christian tradition. Their parents, much less educated for the most part than they, accepted the old traditions without much criticism.

The old forms of religious belief and practice had an almost unchallenged impact upon these students as children during their formative and impressionable years. But as they reached the high schools and particularly the college, they were subjected to an increasingly intensified barrage of scientific and humanistic ideas and facts which influenced their whole outlook. Today, at the end of sixteen or more years of schooling, they find themselves bewildered and searching for a reasonable faith. I suspect they share this state of uncertainty with many of their elders of equivalent education.

Not education, but the state of Western civilization itself, has brought this to pass. The scientific world view has made the authoritarian dogmas of supernatural religion unacceptable to the contemporary mind. Yet the new outlook has failed to satisfy our spiritual needs. Accordingly, while this is a book on education, it is necessarily also a book on religion. I have, however, found it impossible to attack the problem of religion in education without re-examining our religious tradition itself.

In much of the current controversy about the place of religion in public education, all parties make unexamined assumptions about the nature of religion. Generally speaking, both the opponents and the proponents of religion in public education start from the same assumption: that religion can mean nothing else than the supernatural religion of tradition. The argument has the appearance of revolving around the question of whether to exclude religion from or include religion in the program of public education. But what the participants are really debating without explicitly saying so is the adequacy or validity of supernatural religion itself. The more sophisticated of them are aware that this is the case, but both sides have their own reasons for not making the assumption explicit. Since underlying assumptions are not examined, most of the argument is directed at the wrong problems. It seems futile to argue whether the traditional religions are any longer adequate to our age. The question has been settled not by the debaters but by objective changes in Western culture itself. It is equally futile to argue whether religion should be isolated in its own watertight compartment in the student's life. We know this is psychologically unhealthy if not impossible.

The real problem is to find a religious outlook suitable to the modern temper. This outlook, when it emerges, must come from the common life of the people. This book does not presume to predict what the new outlook will be. It rather suggests how education can help people find religious quality in their common experience.

I hope the book will prove valuable to many puzzled people. My own students, graduate and undergraduate, are representative of the kind of persons of all ages and pursuits to whom I would like to address myself. The book does not pretend to provide an explicit religious outlook for the many people whom years of schooling have left stimulated but bewildered. But it does suggest ways of moving so that people can together build their own more common outlook.

The role of the schools in helping our civilization find spiritual direction is a matter of fundamental public policy. I hope the book will be helpful as the people of this nation participate democratically in the determination of this policy. Fortunately, there is a growing number of citizens who are disposed to grapple with such problems in a penetrating, fundamental way before making up their minds. This book may be of use to them, as well as to the educational and religious leaders who rightfully take the lead in stimulating consideration of such questions.

Finally, I hope the book will be of help to those directly involved in guiding the spiritual development of children. While I have written of education, I have not intended to write only of schooling, although many of the examples and references have to do with the latter. I have, rather, thought of education in its broadest sense as the effect of the whole culture, with all its institutions and arrangements, upon the life of the child. Parent, teacher, clergyman, social worker, and many another—each has a role to play in helping the child find his own spiritual fulfilment in the culture of which he is a part.

Yet the teacher does have a special role to play. My own students are examples. Prospective teachers, they are about to enter the classrooms of a great city. Spiritually confused themselves, they will soon be responsible for guiding children who are coming up through the very institution that helped confuse their teachers. This book suggests one approach and point of view from which such teachers can start as they seek to help their children find their own religious meanings.

To avoid confusion, a note is desirable about the concept of "religious modes" employed throughout the book. I see religion as a quality pervasive of all human activity when and if life is carried on creatively at a humane level. All humane living has religious quality, but this quality can be keyed in different moods or modes. For purposes of analysis it has been convenient to distinguish several of these modes and to discuss them separately. But in actuality they are an orchestrated and inseparable part of a single process.

It is not possible to acknowledge properly all my intellectual debts, they are so numerous. It will be obvious how much I owe to the writings of Reinhold Niebuhr, John Dewey, and Henry Nelson Wieman. As for personal help and stimulation, I want to mention first of all Professor Emeritus E. Vern Sayers of the University of Hawaii and Professor George E. Axtelle of New York University, to both of whom I have dedicated this book because their influence upon the growth of my outlook has been so great. Professor Sayers first stimulated in me the ideas that led to the writing of this, while Professor Axtelle worked closely with me all through the project and helped me see it to completion. I am also grateful to Professor Samuel L. Hamilton of the Department of Religious Education, New York University, for his diligent and painstaking criticism of the entire manuscript. Without his help I would have permitted a number of errors and mistaken emphases to reach print. I wish to thank Dr. Ordway Tead of Harper & Brothers for his cogent suggestions, which served to bring the whole manuscript into better focus. Professor Charles A. Seipmann of New York University helped me with matters of expression and presentation. Finally, I wish to express deep gratitude to my wife, Fudeko Tamate Madden, the most severe critic of all, who challenged the content and wording of every page, yet who gave me the encouragement and stimulation I needed to complete this effort. If the book is lacking, it is in spite of, not because of, the help these persons have given me.

WARD MADDEN

Brooklyn, New York
March 1, 1951

Religious Values in Education

CHAPTER I

Introduction

Industrialism, Naturalism, and Supernaturalism

It appears that the next epoch in the history of civilization will be one either of synthesis or of literal and fairly complete atomization. One of the greatest of the many paradoxes created by the industrial character of contemporary civilization is that it both divides and unites us.

A world based on industrialism must be a world based on world-wide planning. Thus we are brought together. The nineteenth century, with its industrial revolution and the rise of nationalism, demonstrated how industrialism brings peoples together to form nations. And now, in the twentieth century, nationalism, once the end point of synthesis, becomes but a steppingstone and, perversely, a stumbling block to still more synthesis. Nations feel drawn together economically into regions and politically into superunits of power. The question whether more than one such center of power can simultaneously exist pushes to the fore, and the ideal of a unified world becomes a matter of life and death.

The forces that unite us also divide us, for out of our technologically ordered society rises the question, Who is to do the planning? This is the fateful question which helps divide the world into armed camps. Those who would place planning—in its broadest social and economic meaning—in the hands of the few are arrayed against those who would find ways by which all those affected by a given plan may participate in its formulation. On the surface this split appears to take place along national lines. We seem confronted by the overwhelming fact of the war of the democracies against the authoritarian nations. But while there is a degree of reality in this appearance, it is a small degree, for not even the democracies have found the constructive, explicit and cooperative democratic answer to the question, Who is to do the planning?

Within the democracies this question produces a split scarcely less disturbing than the one it provokes on an international level. Business, labor, and big government find themselves in conflict with one another. Monopoly capitalism is not the only possible form of capitalism, any more than monopoly practices in labor are the only ways to organize labor, or bureaucracy the only way to organize government. But though monopoly capitalists, dictatorial labor, and bureaucratic government are opposed to one another in most respects, they have one thing in common. They all answer the question, Who is to plan? by assuming that planning should be the prerogative of a special group. Together all three stand in opposition to those who seek the democratic answer. Capital, labor, and government would lose their monopoly characteristics if ways could be found for various interests to participate with one another in determining common goals and mutually acceptable means of social implementation. The democratic faith holds that ways of planning can be found in which all those who will be affected by the plans may participate in a continuing, dynamic and shared process.

Industrialism is stimulating two conflicting movements. On the one hand it is uniting men by making them interdependent; on the other it is dividing men in a struggle for monopoly control of the social growth of international and national economies.

Yet the basis of the race between world synthesis and atomization is not simply a material one. Interpenetrating with the economic base is the ideational base. There are alternative ways to categorize ideas, and it could scarcely be claimed that the conflict of supernaturalism and naturalism is the only way to classify the basic ideas at war in the present struggle for power among and within nations. Yet it can be shown that such a conflict is indeed involved in the issues before us.

To begin with, it must be pointed out that both supernaturalism and naturalism, when they become extreme and one-sided, develop their own characteristic forms of authoritarianism.

Supernaturalism carries the seeds of authoritarianism in its tendency to believe in the existence of absolute being in which all reality, and hence all truth, is embodied. The ordinary man, unable in this life to know absolute being, is asked to accept beliefs about its nature upon the authority of sources which are unwilling or unable to submit their pronouncements and interpretations to the ordinary tests of investigation, inquiry, and validation as these prevail in other aspects of life. There is assumed a body of "revealed" truth which must be accepted unquestioningly, and a hierarchical priesthood which, having alleged special access to truth, acquires power over the minds of men.

Where and when they can, the practitioners of absolutistic supernaturalism do not hesitate directly to control the lives and conduct of men, as in Nazi Germany and Shinto Japan with their pagan supernaturalism, and in Franco Spain with its official Christian supernaturalism. But when, in more democratic countries, direct control of conduct is impossible, an insidious control of the mind by supernaturalistic institutions often remains. Fascism often finds supernaturalism to be a useful bolster to authoritarian control.

Yet naturalism, no less than supernaturalism, bears within itself the possibility of authoritarianism. If supernaturalism has its absolute being, naturalism has its subjective relativism. Naturalism, in its extreme materialistic form, removes every man from subjection to transcendent controlling forces and makes him a law unto himself. The laws of nature—meaning, in this case, the laws of the jungle—prevail, and reliance is placed upon naked, brute force in the control of life, which, as Hobbes put it, becomes "nasty, brutish and short." When subjective values rather than absolute moral law establish the norms of behavior, the world becomes one in which might makes right. Groups of men arise who are bent upon imposing their personal values upon the world. Convinced of the rightness of their values, they argue that the ends justify the means and stop at no outrage upon humanity in order to accomplish these ends.

When and where they can, the practitioners of materialistic authoritarianism do not hesitate to control the lives and conduct of men directly, as in the communist nations. But when direct control of conduct is impossible, as in democratic countries, indirect control through the capitalistic ownership of the means of production may inadvertently result in bringing similar outcomes in less extreme form. Capitalism and communism, symbolizing as they do the conflict of two incompatible worlds, seem strangely to have a common root. Yet the materialism of both is patent.

If the world conflict, whatever else it is, is a conflict between authoritarianism and democracy, we have seemingly found naturalism and supernaturalism aligned together on the side of authoritarianism. We have beaten down the mystical and supernaturally sanctioned authoritarianism of Japan and Hitler only to be confronted by the materialistic authoritarianism of world communism.

Yet there is an opposite side to the picture. Supernaturalism and naturalism both lend themselves also to the support of democratic tendencies. Christianity is a supernatural religion, and the strength of Western democracy stems partly from the humanitarian Christian tradition with its emphasis on the sacredness of the individual and the primary importance of brotherly love. As for naturalism, no more liberalizing influence has operated in Western democracy than science, with its habit of inquiry and its questioning of all authority.

If supernaturalism finds its authoritarian efflorescence in the German and Japanese mystical state, in the Spanish established Church, in the Vatican and elsewhere, it also finds its democratic efflorescence in the Christian ethos, as distinct from the Church. Meanwhile, naturalism becomes authoritarian in the communist state and in monopoly capitalism. But it becomes a foundation of democracy in the scientific outlook which questions and liberates;

in the evolutionary viewpoint which challenges all finalities; in the liberalism which stemmed from Hobbes through Locke to the founders of British and American democracy.

Even on theoretical grounds, both supernaturalism and naturalism oppose authoritarianism as well as support it. If supernaturalism is authoritarian in its insistence on human subjection to fixed and eternal moral law, it is antiauthoritarian in its insistence upon objectively existent rules of conduct as the proper alternative to the ruthless tyranny of the individual who is a law unto himself. And if naturalism can lead to a morality of might, it also, in its relativism, liberates the individual from subjection to eternal absolutes.

It is essential to human survival that the authoritarian elements in both naturalism and supernaturalism be exorcised and destroyed, and that the democratic potentialities in both be cultivated. This means a reconstruction of both the naturalistic and the supernaturalistic points of view, using democracy as the guide by which changes are made. If this is done, the new naturalism and the new supernaturalism will no longer stand opposed and mutually exclusive. Within the framework of democracy they will complement one another in aiding an adequate understanding and control of life and existence.

In terms of technology, the world crisis forces us to recognize that we must plan, but we have not yet solved the problem of who is to plan. In terms of naturalism and supernaturalism, the crisis is a situation in which extreme and one-sided views have led to absolutisms which support authoritarian answers to the question of who is to plan.

The Need for Synthesis

Significantly, even while the authoritarian countries move toward new extremes of materialism on the one side or supernaturalism on the other, the democratic countries show signs of movement in the direction of a naturalistic-supernaturalistic synthesis. Historically religion, supernaturalism, and idealism have done the most justice to the creativity in the universe and life, while materialism has done most justice to the natural cause-and-effect relations by which change becomes less mysterious and more explicable. But whereas once we saw a conflict between creativity and mechanistic determinism, we are now beginning to see mind and purpose as emergent qualities in a cause-and-effect but not predetermined universe.

The frontier edge of the American mentality has outgrown the oversimplified materialism of Newtonian physics, Watsonian psychology, and the acquisitive society, without, however, losing the tough-mindedness of the earlier outlook. We have reached the point where naturalistic philosophers examine myth, not merely for its symbolism, but for its essential truth; and where some religious philosophers and theologians, such as Henry Nelson Wieman and Reinhold Niebuhr, produce writings that seem intolerably naturalistic to their more traditional-minded critics. In America the naturalism of the leading philosophers has seemed a fruition of the naturalism common to the American mentality. Significantly, John Dewey has seemed to his materialistic-minded critics to be tainted with philosophical idealism, while his idealistic critics see him as a materialist. A new naturalism and a new supernaturalism are both emerging, each, as it moves beyond the reductionism and one-sidedness of its ancestry, growing closer to the other.

Yet the synthesis has scarcely begun—the big jobs remain to be done. This is especially true at the point that really matters—in the life and conduct of the ordinary man. He continues to live in a world split between the uninspired secularism of the workaday world and the sterile spirituality reserved for Sundays at a given hour.

The secularism of the public school is one of the characteristic manifestations of this state of affairs. This situation in the schools is both praised and condemned, depending on which side of the fence the observer stands. On the one hand, we are told that the schools are the Godless instrument of Satan; that naturalism is the only "sect" permitted access to the schools. On the other hand, alarms are sounded to the effect that organized religion is out to recapture the schools, and we are told this would mean the smothering of the American mentality by authoritarianism and a prescientific outlook.

Of the immediate causes of secularism in the public schools, the most important has been sectarianism. The principle of the separation of Church and State originated, not because of antipathy for religion, but because each sect sought protection from the domination of every other sect. The colonial schools and the schools of the early Republic were essentially religious schools, and there was no widespread serious intention that they should be otherwise. The first amendment to the Constitution and the various state constitutions sought to preserve the right of the people to choose between alternative religious views or to remain unreligious if they so chose. The legal effect of these provisions was, and remains, with the exception of laws in some states, one of excluding sectarian teaching, but not necessarily religion, from the public schools. But the practical effect has been to exclude religion itself. There has never been agreement sufficient to make the teaching of a common core of religious belief possible.

But the causes of secularism in the schools go even deeper. The schools are secular essentially because contemporary society itself is secular. There are three basic and related trends, aside from sectarianism, which have helped produce our secular civilization and which must be reckoned with in any attempt to make a new approach to religion and education. These are the development of modern science, the rise of democracy, and the belief in the integral relation of mind and body.

If we accept—and it appears that we must—the basic meaning of these three developments, then we will have to share the common skeptical attitude toward much that has been traditional in religion. The first two of these—science and democracy—are a challenge to all authoritarianism in religion and to all claims to full acquaintance with ultimate truth. The third—the belief in the integral relation of mind and body—makes it impossible any longer to think of a world of spirit which is different in kind and separable from the corporeal world.

The acceptance of these ideas confronts us with a choice—shall we reject religion altogether and continue in our secular ways, or shall we seek a reconstruction of the meaning of religion compatible with the democratic-scientific outlook?

It seems strategically important that the second choice—the reconstruction of our religious outlook—be made at this time of crisis. There are two compelling reasons.

In the first place, we are in desperate need of moral and spiritual commitments capable of mobilizing our energies for making a better world. Men of all persuasions recognize this, and each, whether fascist, communist, democrat, or Christian, tries in his own way to meet the need. Though some of these ways are immeasurably better than others, none has proved good enough—a new effort is needed.

In the second place, it is the better part of strategy to make use of the resources we have already developed. Traditional religious outlooks represent judgments based upon ages of religious experience. They command the deepest loyalties of millions of persons. Rather than start with a clean slate, it seems better to make use of the generations of experience and the loyalties which may be used as springboards toward a religious way of life appropriate to the scientific, democratic, organismic outlook of our age.

The Religious Quality of Experience

What direction should the reconstruction of religion take?

First of all a distinction should be made between religion as a quality of experience and religion as a structure of special doctrine. A man's conduct may have in it a quality which we recognize as religious even when allegiance by him to a formal religion is lacking, or even when he is antagonistic to formal religions, to all religious dogma, and to all cultic practices.

As a quality of experience, religion is a phenomenon to be looked for in the daily productive activities of men as they carry on their various occupations and pursuits. Such activities have religious quality when they are conducted wholeheartedly with insight into their significance and faith in their worth-whileness.

The religious person in this sense is the one who characteristically approaches life situations with an implicit faith that, no matter how good or bad these may be, something can be done to improve them. To be religious is to live with faith in the transformability of existence for the better.

The irreligious attitude, in contrast, is the approach to life in a spirit of cynicism or futility. Not that the religious attitude consists of sentimental insistence that what seems bad is really good, or that conditions will by accident somehow adjust themselves for the better. The improvement of life demands a tough realism in recognizing bad things for what they are, and in perceiving clearly the obstacles to productive activity. There are times when such realism must generate feelings of despair. But there are no times when cynicism is called for. Cynicism marks the end of constructive activity. Instead, situations can be approached with a fundamentally positive spirit in which there is determination to find some way to make things better or at least less bad.

The man with religious quality in his conduct is not immune to despair. He has no blind faith in the inevitable upward trend of human progress. He feels that the realization of his destiny is conditional upon his own efforts, which may fail. Nevertheless, he lives his life in a spirit of fundamental buoyancy and optimism. His buoyancy grows out of what may be called his cosmic perspective. He realizes that even though the improvement of life is dependent upon his own efforts, still the good things in life are not solely of his own making. He recognizes his continuity with the rest of humanity both in geographic space and in history, and his continuity with nature. He knows that while his relation to nature and to humanity creates all his problems, it also provides the resources by which those problems may be attacked. He is in league with the rest of the universe. His problems are not those of a lonely individual confronted by an alien and terrifying universe, but rather those of an individual who sees himself as a part of the universe, facing with it its own internal and intrinsic problems.

When a man lives his life in such a way that he is able to see his activities in their creative relation to the activities of other men, his behavior gains religious quality. Any conduct carried on with a concern for improving the goodness or quality of life has religious spirit, but the desirability of any given activity cannot be assayed except in its relation to other activities. The goodness of life depends upon the willingness of men to choose activities which integrate with the activities of other men—which are socially constructive and reciprocally productive activities. There is perspective and a sense of values in the life of the man who acts religiously.

The life of such a man has purposive quality. It is commonly recognized that life to be good must have a purpose, and the established religions are alleged to give life that purpose. For the structured religions, indeed, life not sanctioned by them can have no purpose. But we commonly recognize that men who give allegiance to no established religion, not even to religion in principle, often lead rich and purposeful lives. We realize, in fact, that such lives *are* their religion—we say of a man, for example, that his pusuit of science or his devotion to living a democratic life constitutes his religion.

Religion in this sense is a dedication of the entire self to the pursuit of ideal values. One's ideals, in this case, are not permitted to become a decoration crowning the rest of life, or a set of goals, the pursuit of which is confined to special activities set aside or designated for that purpose. Rather all life activities are in such lives evaluated and directed in terms of their coherence with the ideals which come to illuminate their meaning.

In order to be good, life activities must be integrated with the creative activities of other men. Religious quality exists in the conduct of a man who continually expands the scope of the community which he recognizes as his own until it takes in all humanity and all history. In a sense he loses his ego in community; yet, paradoxically, by doing so he finds himself and strengthens his individual selfhood. He finds his unique and distinctive role in society by becoming more social. He enriches his individuality by partaking of what society in all its variety can contribute to him when he is a conscious and cooperating part of it.

The religious man displays these modes of living not because he is religious; rather, by operating in these modes, he becomes religious. Religious quality, whether it is labeled as such or not, develops in the life and experience of the individual as he integrates his values with one another and with those of society, as he dedicates his life to the reconstruction of values to make them more ideal, as he devotes himself to the realization of his ideals, as he recognizes his communal relation to society, and as he finds a productive role to play in society.

Religion as a structure of special doctrine has often inhibited the development of religious quality in life and experience. Its tendency to focus man's attention upon an unknowable supernatural world has diverted his energies from the task of improving the quality of actual life and existence. The rigidity of its structures has stifled rather than released his creativity. It has placed claims upon him which, far from enlarging his sense of community and helping him approach the world with an open and generous attitude, have often made him a tower of arrogance, intolerant of his fellow man.

Religion in the Public School

The distinction between the religious quality of experience and the structured doctrinaire religions provides a base for a new approach to the problem of religion in the public schools. Making this distinction enables us to to strengthen the American tradition of separation of Church and State, while at the same time we engage in the intensive cultivation of religious quality in the educational experience of our children.

The principle of separation of Church and State should continue, as it has done from its inception, to keep structured religion out of the public schools. The child cannot be permitted to fall into the hands of those who would be more interested in selling him a "bill of goods" than in developing his critical skills and ability to make a reasoned judgment of his own. Structured religion by its very nature is obligated to secure a grip upon the mind of the child at the earliest possible moment. From the point of view of the religious groups involved, it has an imperious missionary function to perform. But this tends to throw religion into opposition to the primary goal of American education, which is the promotion of the spirit of freedom and equality which are the hallmarks of American democracy. The way to freedom is to develop in our citizens the habits and skills of practical judgment which enable them to make up their own minds both as to social policy and to the conduct of their personal lives. The way to equality is to foster respect for individual differences and to value differences for the contribution and stimulation they can give to the activities and ideas of society. For children to stop thinking or for differences to give way to conformity would be intolerable. The interests of structured religion are such that it is bound to throw its weight in opposition to the fundamental educational goals of helping children learn to think for themselves and to encourage and value differences among the members of society.

But even while the door of the school is closed in the face of creedal religion, the school should undertake a responsibility it has thus far evaded—the cultivation of religious quality in the experience of children.

In order to do this, a setting is required in which children live and work together. Two essential elements in such a setting are that the children work on problems which have grown out of their own experience and are of common concern to them, and that the work be organized on the basis of cooperative group living. Learning is essentially a process of problem-solving. But the problems must be recognized by the children as genuine to them—as problems that have arisen as disturbances in their already ongoing activities.

And the attack upon problems is more productive if the resources of an entire group are brought to bear. Learning to work with others is itself a basic educational objective, and it provides the opportunity to learn to live and practice democracy.

In such a setting, religious quality can be helped to emerge in the activities of the group. Religious quality refers to the spirit in which the children carry on their various pursuits. As the children proceed with their work, planning it, organizing it, making choices as to what to do and how to do it, they will find that various values are involved which come into conflict with one another. As such disturbances arise, the children need help in understanding and interpreting what is at stake. Here is the beginning of the development of a sense of values. As the process is carried further, a growing set of ideal values emerges from the children's experiences. The teacher serves as aid in helping children analyze, evaluate, and integrate the values involved. As the children mature, they make their own commitments to the ideals to which they choose to dedicate their life conduct.

Furthermore, as the work of the children proceeds, they discover that many of the values involved in the process are social values. They recognize that success is not solely of their own individual making, but is the result of how well the group learns to plan, think, and work together. They can be helped to see their relationship to their culture and to nature, and to sense the degree to which they draw upon the resources of both in promoting their activities. From such experiences can grow a sense of community and of the individual's relation to the community.

In short, there can develop in the experience of the children a spirit of dedication of the self to carefully considered ideals, to the processes of inquiry which produce those ideals, and to the creative powers of the community through which the self realizes itself.

Distinguishing the religious quality of experience from structured religion would strengthen the hand of American democracy in its effort to keep structured religion out of the public schools. Many persons fear, with good grounds, that organized religion is gathering momentum in its effort to make inroads upon public education. The strength of organized religion's position rests partly on the growing feeling in America that important and effective steps must indeed be taken in cultivating the spiritual life of the child. But until religious quality is disentangled from structured religion, the latter will ride into the schools on the coattails of the former. If the distinction is made, the growing and valid demand for spiritual education can be satisfied without endangering traditional freedoms.

Toward Religious Reconstruction

If American teachers are seriously to undertake the cultivation of religious quality in the activities of children, they will have to learn to identify the modes of conduct that have religious quality and to distinguish them from the special religious structures prevalent in our culture. This requires nothing less than a reorganization of one's religious outlook, with special attention to the conditions imposed upon such an outlook by the demands of the democratic-scientific-organismic outlook of our age.

With this in mind, the present task is to analyze and identify the nature of the religious quality and to suggest how it can be cultivated in the activities of children.

First, an examination of the religious life of man, in order to identify the characteristics of the religious quality, will be undertaken. The problem is to strip away the trappings of structured religion and to find the religious spirit which actually pervades the affairs of everyday life. In doing this we will be exploring material which is so associated with a one-sided supernatural context as to make it unacceptable in its unreconstructed form to many enlightened minds.

For this reason it will seem to many that the material is not even promising, and that a start had better be made elsewhere. But to adopt such an attitude would be to rule out in advance the possibility that in the experience of the human race are to be found religious resources which, while they are badly in need of reconstruction, can stimulate in the modern mind insights which might otherwise be missed. It is conceivable that our supernatural-minded ancestors struggled for insights that they grasped only vaguely and could express only symbolically. To ignore their spadework, even though much further work remains to be done, would be a waste of resources.

Furthermore, there is a strategy required of any generation such as our own, if it would succeed in its purpose of building new ways of life. To build, one must have materials, and the only materials available to us in building a way of life are those which constitute culture and tradition. Reorganized and reconstituted the materials must be, but they provide the starting point.

In order to overcome the supernatural bias of the materials dealt with in any examination of our religious heritage, the tools of the modern social sciences should be used. In the following pages the religious life of man is examined from a sociological and psychological point of view. The aim is to discover the psychosocial needs that man satisfies through his religious practices, and to see how these practices might be modified both so that they meet the needs in question more adequately and so that they meet them in a way which is not only compatible with but positively supports our contemporary scientific habits of mind and democratic concepts of good human relations.

The Religious Modes

Men conduct their lives in varying moods which flow continuously into one another. We move from boredom into elation, from elation into despair, from despair into hopefulness, into and out of a thousand other moods as the dramatic plot involved in living our lives spins itself out from day to day. All our daily occupations, whether they consist of resting, playing, or working, are pervaded by one mood or another. Our moods manifest themselves in ways of doing things. We work at this or that task diligently or sluggishly, creatively or mechanically, according to the dominant mood of that time. We have modes of conduct which accompany corresponding moods. Any given mode is the active counterpart of a mood; any given mood is the passive counterpart of some mode of conduct.

Religion is here interpreted as essentially a mode or mood which may hopefully characterize our common, daily occupations and activities. It is a quality which can become present in the way we do everyday things. Yet, as subsequent analysis will seek to show, it is a mode compounded of many other modes. It is an orchestration of many modes which, taken together as integrated parts of a whole, constitute the religious way of living as contrasted to unspirited or dispirited ways of conducting ordinary affairs.

In the following pages several of the modes, moods, or aspects of effort and aspiration which together constitute the religious quality of experience are identified, described, and analyzed. Though they cannot in the actuality of daily living be separated from one another, they are treated one at a time under their somewhat arbitrarily designated labels. These religious modes, as explicated in successive chapters, are, in the order of presentation, the *valuational,* the *community*, the *executive*, the *aesthetic*, and the *contemplative* modes. We begin with the valuation mode.

CHAPTER II

The Valuational Mode: Origin and Development

MAN is born into a world of good and evil, not one of neutral fact. The infant's life is one crisis after another—the shock of emergence from the womb, the fight for the first breath, the demand for nutrition, sleep, activity. Early infancy is a confusion of events out of which consciousness gradually fixes upon the visage of the first god—the beneficent and omnipotent parent. Without accepting the dictum of the Freudian that this is the last god,[1] we perhaps can accept it as a first one and as a beginning toward understanding the last one.

The values we recognize emerge in our active relationship with the world. Our interests, needs, goals, and even our moral judgments come into existence and enter consciousness only as we take hold of and deal with our world.

But the mere using of objects in the environment, the mere liking and disliking of them, does not in itself account for the consciousness of value, least of all in the religious sense. Such consciousness begins to emerge when a social group and the individuals in it begin to organize themselves about the objects and ideas to which they must attend and which they must prize or value as they seek to improve the quality of life. There is a deliberate and conscious organization into a way of life—into a culture, as far as

[1] See "Totem and Taboo" in *The Basic Writings of Sigmund Freud*, pp. 919-920.

the group goes, and into a personality related to the culture, as far as the individual goes. A set of conventional standards and social arrangements is built by the group, which defines it as a society; a set of habits is built by the individual, which defines him as an individual.

The values that originate in mere impulsive action have to be integrated; and in becoming an organized whole they undergo a change of content which makes their relationship to their humble origins all but unrecognizable. This is why a single term like "love" can be used to refer to phenomena as far removed from one another as the infant's animal response to its mother and the Christian's spiritual response to humanity.

Magic to Religion: From Ejaculatory to Pervasive Values

The natural history of man's religious development is in effect a record of his maturing conception of value, that is, what he cherishes as of great worth. Man first experiences value as a mere ejaculatory discharge of emotion at the moment he likes or dislikes this or that immediate experience. His explanations of the good and bad things that befall him are little more than magical explanations, and he uses magic to strive to insure more of the good things and less of the bad. But as he matures he consolidates and integrates values with one another. They become more pervasive, refined, and coherent in their totality. Explanations that once seemed merely magical or capricious begin to take on that quality which we can soundly recognize as religious. Magical incantations intended to bring about some limited result begin to take on the quality of religious ritual aimed at the realization of deeper, more pervasive values.

Some analysis of what happens in this process in its origins will throw light upon the fundamental nature of religion.

We can start with an example.[2] A West African fisherman col-

[2] The example is taken by Irving King in *The Development of Religion*, p. 56, from R. H. Nassau, *Fetichism in West Africa* (New York: 1904, pp. 83-84).

lects with care the ingredients of a concoction which he boils over a fire. He sits with his face in the steam rising from the pot and speaks into the pot, "Let me catch fish every day! Every day!" He takes the pot off the fire, not with his hands, but with his feet, eats, and calls a dog to finish what is left. He strikes the eating dog sharply, saying, "So may I strike the fish!" He kicks the pot over, leaves it until night, when he returns to dash it violently to the ground, saying, "So may I kill fish." All this must be accomplished without discovery by any other villager. The phrases used, the effect of the solitude and the danger of discovery, the difficulty of the way in which each step has to be performed, build up an emotional tension which centers upon the value of the act of fishing itself.

Psychologically, this is what is happening to the fisherman: he is getting himself "set" for the task to be done. He is mobilizing his energies in readiness for the effort required to realize a particular and important value.

Many instances like the foregoing are familiar in primitive society.[3] In such examples one can discern man organizing himself at a prereligious level about a value in a way that anticipates at a higher level of sophistication the emergence of religious consciousness. These instances involve a complicated array of accompaniments to basic economic activities. The hunter, the fisherman, the housebuilder, use a certain language instead of the everyday language in talking of their planned activity; they wear certain kinds of clothing and use certain kinds of implements and materials, though to an outsider it might appear that other kinds might serve the purpose as well; they recite certain formulas and perform certain ritualistic ceremonies thought to ensure success.

Without knowing why he does these things, the primitive man accomplishes a focusing of his consciousness upon the realizing of the values involved. There is a spiritual girding up of the loins in preparation for the rigors of practical activity. The use of certain kinds of leaves rather than others to build a bird-hunting blind may well have originated by accident when the first use of one kind was

[3] Some of these have been brought together by King, *op. cit.*, pp. 47-61.

accompanied by success and that of another was not. But to use the leaf one's ancestors found successful serves a psychological purpose in providing the faith in success which helps ensure success. Not only does one know that this is what others did to succeed, but in addition he feels a sustaining kinship with those others, his ancestors.

Such examples may well strike us as being more illustrative of magic than of religion. But they are the raw stuff out of which religion—and science as well—has been born. Magic as practiced by primitive man is an effort to realize certain cherished values, an effort to bring about certain desired results. Magic could evolve into science only as more realistic ways of ascertaining the connection between cause and effect developed. But magic is an expression of the desire to control or predict the outcome of an event by attending to its causes. This concern with cause-and-effect connections is, moreover, the dominant motif of experimental science.

As in the movement from magic to science, the movement from magic to religion requires an enormous maturing of experience and insight. The values which magic seeks to realize are narrow and utilitarian, as when water is sprinkled to produce a shower. Or they represent egocentric values, as when the fingernail parings of an enemy are collected in order to hold magic dominion over his body.

When men integrate many particular values into an overarching whole, when they unite the partial and private values of separate individuals to form pervasive values having social significance, then the accompanying rituals that once seemed mere magical incantations begin to gain religious quality. The difference between magic and religion is exemplified in the difference between an incantation carried out to prevent death in childbed and a rite in celebration of a birth. The former has a definite and particular aim; the latter appears to have no end beyond itself—it seems rather to express the feelings of the community about the worth of childbearing without seeking to bring about any specific behavior in the future.

The anthropologist finds that religious acts bring to the community a consciousness of itself as a group and of its destiny. They serve to establish and enhance a valuable mental attitude—a commitment to a value essential to the life of the group. Childbearing as a general function transcends in social importance the bearing of any particular child. The coming of a particular child can even be a misfortune, but not the general fact, at least in the days before overpopulation became a problem. The worth of events like childbearing is certified to by the experience of the group rather than by the egocentric and momentary desires of the single individual. Such certification appears in the guise of tradition and custom, which stabilize the values in question. Through custom and tradition one becomes united with his people in loyalty to common values.

Conception, pregnancy, birth, puberty, marriage, death, are among the crises in life when existence is filled with hope or despair. No wonder religion, as concerned with the preservation and extension of value, is particularly associated with these times and is expressed in such rituals as christening, confirmation, initiation, marriage, ministering to the sick, and burial. Any one of these rituals can illustrate the fact that religion, as distinct from the immature ejaculations associated with magic, expresses a maturation of man's value-consciousness and concern.

Take, for example, the initiation ceremony at puberty. The intent of that ceremony is to transmit to the novitiate the traditions, lore, and knowledge of the tribe, and to impress them indelibly through seclusion and ordeal. The values involved are deep, pervasive, and social; not momentary, partial, and private. The very survival of the tribe as such depends upon the success of this, its effort to transmit and preserve its culture. No wonder that the sanction of a supreme power is appealed to, and that the ceremony is associated with the idea of the death and rebirth of the novitiate. His spiritual death as a child and his rebirth as a man are necessary both for his own salvation and for that of the tribe. This necessary new status is accomplished through his assimilation of the deepest values by which the tribe lives.

The Deification of Values: From Momentary Gods to Polytheism

The emergence of religion represents a growth in the power to integrate limited values into basic life values. This is evidenced in the evolution of the idea of deity. There is a movement from momentary and partial deities, which symbolize the impulsive disliking and liking of the moment, to departmental or functional deities, which symbolize the tested value of established types of occupation and activity, and finally to monotheism, which is the result of integrating and universalizing values in a way that enables them to be regarded as supreme.[4]

Momentary[5] or spontaneous gods represent the untested value claims of the experience of the moment unrelated to the whole fabric of experience and value. A man looking for water drives his machete into the damp soil of a likely looking hollow and is confronted by the welling up of gory-looking water. He persuades his family to come and worship it. The red water clears, but from that time it is a divinity to its discoverer and his kin. Another man takes refuge from an enemy in an anthill and afterward says, "The anthill saved my life." Again, a man who happens to be standing beneath a certain breadfruit tree feels an inexplicable fear. He takes his fright to be a sign that the tree is a divinity who wants to live with and be worshipped by him.[6] Any fear, desire, wish, or other passing emotion can be objectified in consciousness as the presumed image of a momentary deity.

Although momentary gods represent untested value claims, they nevertheless play an important role in the growth of man's powers of valuation. By symbolizing a value claim, they make possible the

[4] Ernst Cassirer, *Language and Myth*, pp. 18-20. The opposed theory, that monotheism is the original version of deity, championed primarily by Father Wilhelm Schmidt, is not well accepted by anthropologists. See Schmidt, *The Origin and Growth of Religion*.

[5] The concept of momentary deity is adapted by Cassirer from Spieth, *Die Religion der Eweer in Sud-Togo* (Leipzig, 1911).

[6] The examples are taken by Cassirer, *op. cit.*, pp. 22-23, from Spieth, *op. cit.*, pp. 7 ff.

holding on to a value once experienced while it is imaginatively projected into the future to test its coherence with other values and its adequacy as a guide to further conduct. Symbolic expression makes possible the retrospect and prospect which characterize intelligence. By means of symbols, ideas and values are fixed in consciousness. Language itself, man's primary instrument of reflective behavior, is a form of symbolization. But the nonlinguistic symbolization involved in such activities as imagery, art, and religion serves to express meanings that can only be felt, not intellectualized.[7] Even though a momentary god originates as a mere spasmodic emotion, he became substantial through symbolization. His image remains in the primitive mind long after the specific fear, wish, or hope that generated him has disappeared from memory.[8]

If he can stand the test of further experience, the momentary god may rise to be a functional god.[9] Functional gods symbolize values which, while they may have originated as spontaneous animal feeling, enter into the ordered and continual activities of men. Nearly every department of human activity has given rise to a deity that serves as its patron. When a value, first symbolized as a momentary god, has its meaning enriched and modified by the experience of generations of men, it becomes a functional god. The momentary gods that survive and grow in importance are those which symbolize values essential to the life of the people.

Thus there are fishing gods for sea peoples, fertility gods for agriculturists, rain gods for those living in dry areas, war gods for those living among enemies.[10] Whole pantheons of gods spring up which in their aggregate symbolize the values embodied in all the basic social and economic activities of a given people. The Society

[7] See Susanne Langer, *Philosophy in a New Key,* for a treatment of the importance of the symbolic mode in experience.

[8] Cassirer, *op. cit.,* pp. 35-36.

[9] The term "functional" is here used to include any deity which is associated with some department of human activity, whether he is a member of a pantheon or not.

[10] See Joachim Wach, *Sociology of Religion,* pp. 205-286, for a survey of the relationships between socioeconomic activities and the religious beliefs and practices of various peoples and groups.

Islanders have gods of husbandry, carpentry, forest work, acting, singing, hairdressing, and others; the Samoans have fruit, fish, rain, and healing gods; the New Zealanders war, marine, food, and peace gods.

As civilizations advance, social and economic values continue to be symbolized religiously. The samurai of Japan take the essentially peaceful virtues symbolized in Buddhism and modify them so that they express the warlike virtues. The trade and craft guilds of early China, Japan, and India, and of medieval Europe develop their own patron deities and saints, symbolizing the value of the particular economic activity over which each presides.

Yet such examples, all at the level of polytheism, illustrate only partially integrated values. Fragmentary and private values are grouped in departments having broad social significance, and are symbolized by fragmented deities or patrons of all sorts. Man at this level has grown valuationally—he has learned to relate values to one another and to distinguish those that are enduring and significant from those that are transitory and ejaculatory. Yet at this stage he still has his basic values sealed in separate compartments. That he is capable of further integration of his basic social, economic, personal, and ethical values is demonstrated in the rise of monotheism, the significance of which is analyzed in the next chapter.

CHAPTER III

The Integration and Differentiation of Value

The Maturation of Value-Consciousness

As the religious consciousness matures, it tends to move from polytheism, with its pantheons of functional gods, through many transitions to the monotheism which characterizes most of the great world religions. An analysis of the nature of maturation in valuation will help explain this phenomenon.

As men mature, they tend to integrate and universalize the values by which they live.

A young child, for example, reacts to whatever value claim is in the forefront of his consciousness without realization that acting upon it may create a situation which will restrict the range of values toward which subsequent acts can be directed. He is too inexperienced to see how his acts affect one another. He responds to situations in their immediacy, seeking to realize values which he has failed to see in their potentially destructive or supporting relation to other values in which he may also find himself interested. His world is one of numerous unrelated and often conflicting values, and his acts are responses to whichever of these values is pushed into his consciousness by the circumstances of the moment.

His difficulty is a lack of experience, and a failure to make use of his experiences to bring his various values into coherent relationship with one another. The achievement of self-control in the maturing individual is not simply a matter of learning to suppress one impulse so that something more important may later be realized. Self-control results rather from a process of learning from experience how values affect one another when they are acted upon. It results from a process of modifying and reorganizing values so that they support rather than cancel out one another. Insofar as the individual profits from experience, he learns to keep his whole world of values, or a large part of it, in mind and to direct his acts in such a way that as much of the whole as possible is supported by a given act in order that the individual may preserve a sense of his own wholeness or unity. He learns not to permit a partial value to rule him without examination of its relation to the rest of his prized values.

The mark of maturity is the integration of values into a consistent and coherent value structure. We associate maturity with experience because experience shows the intrinsic relations among values.

The foregoing holds true both for individuals and societies. The individual develops a personal sense of values, integrated in experience, which help to guide his life. A society develops an ideology which becomes part of its culture and represents value integrations growing out of successive generations of acceptable human experience. If gods symbolize values, monotheism represents a maturing of the valuational aspects of a society or culture, in which the partial and unintegrated values formerly symbolized by pantheons of fragmented gods, having now become integrated, are symbolized by a single god. We will return to this idea later.

An accompaniment of the integration of values is the tendency of each individual value to extend itself to become universal rather than remain limited and particular. As each value is reconstructed and built into the growing value structure, its meaning is expanded through its relation to the totality of which it is a part. It becomes a value no longer limited and partial in application, but one which has a pervasive influence in the lives of those who accept it. As long as a value remains unintegrated with other values in the consciousness of an immature person or society, it can rule conduct only at restricted and discrete times and places. As circumstances change, another value, disparate with and possibly contradictory to the first, may take over.

But when a value can become part of an integrated value structure, it tends to become consistent with more and more aspects of the individual's total life behavior. While an integrated value cannot, any more than can an unintegrated one, rule conduct under all circumstances, nevertheless an integrated value, as it falls temporarily into the background, is not contradicted by whatever other value becomes more relevant in another situation. Each one of an integrated set of values is still consistent with behavior even when some other value in the set comes forward to influence behavior temporarily.

In a sense, however, each one of an integrated value structure *does* control behavior at all times and all places. Even when another member of the structure is the dominant controlling value at the moment, all other values in the structure are part of the total controlling core of values. Unintegrated values, if they happen to contradict one another, lose all control the moment circumstances change and one value rather than another takes over. But in the case of integrated values, the only problem raised when one situation replaces another is not which value is to control at the expense of another, but rather which value of many related ones is the most relevant at the moment.

Values, then, tend to become universal as they become incorporated with and integrated into one another. This does *not* mean that they become absolute, eternal, and unchangeable. On the contrary, the whole concept of values as products of experience and as related to one another through living experience emphasizes the continuous reconstruction and reintegration both of individual values and of the over-all structure in which they become united. For a value to become universal means that, as part of a total integrated value structure, it is guiding conduct for the individual at all times and places. But the totality with its parts responds to the reconstruction demanded by experience.

The Expansion of Good Through Integregation

The integration and universalizing of value have both a consummatory and an ethical aspect. Values are good both in the sense of that which consummates or satisfies, and in the sense of that which is ethical or right.

Man is concerned with the continual expansion of consummated and achieved good. The test of the goodness of an act or experience lies in its means-ends or cause-and-effect relation to other acts or experiences.[1] We are driven to modify and redefine a given value when we perceive the things it leads to or does not lead to when acted upon, and when we consider the things that must be done in order to realize or fulfill it. Modification of a given value may be needed to bring it into coherent relationship with the values involved both in the steps leading to it and in the consequences stemming from it. Such consideration of steps and consequences is essentially what is involved in the re-evaluation of values. The more that particular values are thus investigated and brought into relationship with other values, the more the individual is achieving a coherent and unified system of values.

Ethically, the progressive integration of value represents an improvement in the relations of men with one another. Through experience man senses, and even consciously learns, that the good of the individual and the good of society are inseparably linked one with another. He reaches a point where he can no longer ask himself the question whether a given act brings good consequences to himself without asking himself also whether the act brings good consequences to others. He becomes aware of a demand to consider the good of others as well as his own good, and thus his value judgments extend out to become ethical judgments.

As men become concerned with the good of one another, the values that demand to be incorporated into the individual's growing structure of value represent not only claims made by the indi-

[1] This is the key concept in the experimental conception of valuation. See John Dewey, *Theory of Valuation*, pp. 1-67.

vidual but also claims made by others. There tends imperiously to be an integration of not only his limited personal values but a widened integration of the values of all men. Such integration is made possible by the participation and communication of men with one another, and becomes a part of their culture.

Insofar as a man's life throws him into participative relations with others, he shares the experience of others. The distinction between values growing out of his personal experience and values growing out of the experiences of others becomes blurred. The sharing of experience makes the question "whose experience?" irrelevant for him. The other's experience becomes his own experience. Hence the question of "whose values?" becomes equally irrelevant. When the individual encounters a conflict of values, he no longer settles the conflict in favor of his personal values at the expense of the other. Instead he feels the same demand for integration of the two values that is created whenever there is a competition of value claims in his own personal experience.

The pressure of this psychological demand has led to some variant of the Golden Rule becoming the basic ethical principle of all the world religions. It becomes a matter of ethics that a man refuse to claim a value for himself unless he is willing for all others to make the same claim. Kant stated this as the categorical imperative: "Act only on that maxim whereby thou canst at the same time will that it should become a universal law."[2] The categorical imperative points out that universality is the necessary condition of a value claim's being admitted to the status of value. I cannot proclaim for myself the right to steal unless I am willing for all men to have that right. Unless we are willing that a given value be held by all men, we cannot recognize its validity. The categorical imperative is accepted by the individual when and if experience teaches him the interrelatedness of all values.

Thus there are two principles—the coherence principle and the categorical imperative—which complement one another in the effort to universalize values. The coherence principle draws at-

[2] Immanuel Kant, *Ethics*.

tention to the need of uncovering through experience the relations between values so that they may be reconstructed and integrated with one another to create a consistent universe of good. The categorical imperative draws attention to the ethical aspect of this process—draws attention to the demand to consider the needs and interests of all men, the value claims in the experience of others as one seeks integration in valuing and in values. The coherence principle makes values universal in the sense of being related to one another, while the categorical imperative makes values universal in the sense of answering deeply to the needs and demands of all men.

From Polytheism Toward Monotheism

Polytheism is a stage in human development at which the many values rising within experience are still contending with one another. Polytheism is a correctly directed but incomplete effort to organize and stabilize the values motivating the lives of a given people. But as civilizations advance, men more clearly grasp the relations of values to one another, and a coalescence of their gods begins.

The values of the members of a society grow out of the activities and pursuits of their common life, and the unification of their values accompanies a more coherent organizing of their entire social life and culture. They become conscious of themselves as a people having a common heritage and common aspirations.

As expressed in terms of the development of the gods, the process often begins with one member of a pantheon rising to a position of supremacy and embodying in himself a wide range of value. When the unity of a people is still loose, and values are still fighting for prestige, as in Greece, a dominant god such as Zeus may have a rebellious gang of lesser gods on his hands. But as a people becomes united around a national or ethical ideal, as among the Hebrews, a dominant god such as Jahweh may achieve a much higher order of supremacy over the lesser gods. He incorporates into himself the values they formerly symbolized. The movement from many gods to one is for most peoples a slow, tortuous process, reflecting the struggle of the competing values in their experience, and the difficulty of finding coherence in the chaos of conflicting values that assail man. But as a society stabilizes its values, the dominant god embodies the basic values by which the society becomes conscious of itself and its role in history.

Often, as the values of a society integrate, the people begin to say that the various gods in their pantheon are simply different appearances of one and the same god. They hold that there is one god who in many different guises bears different names. This leads to the phenomenon of polynomy, in which a deity, uniting in himself a wealth of attributes that originally belonged to the functional gods which are his components, bears all the names of the latter. Thus in the Koran, Allah appears as the hundred-named, and in Egyptian writings the goddess Isis appears as the thousand-named, the ten-thousand-named. Furthermore, the power of such a god is regarded as in direct proportion to the number of his names. In other words, he embodies a range of value, the extent of which is indicated by the number of gods he has incorporated into himself.

The Demand for Coherence and Universality

The men in history who led the way from polytheism to monotheism were either the moral or the intellectual leaders of their time—the kind of men one would expect to find most sensitive to lack of coherence among values and most determined to make them coherent.

The great Jewish prophets were of the first—the ethical—type. The logic of the connection between valuational coherence and monotheism is expressed in the fact that the two things for which the prophets are most noted are their demand for universal social justice and their struggle to put a single and universal god upon a firm and unchallengeable basis.

Amos denounced the Israelites for an economy in which the

power of wealth was used to oppress the lower classes. Mere worship without righteousness revolted him; he demanded that there be not burnt offerings but social justice, not oblations but uprightness and kindness. And a few years later Isaiah was crying out, "Your hands are full of blood! Wash you, make you clean, take your evil doings out of my sight; leave off doing evil, learn to do well; strive after justice, punish the oppressor, do justice to the orphan, defend the cause of the widow.[3]

This ethical and valuational maturity of the prophets was accompanied by their efforts to make Jahweh the one and only god, supreme and unchallenged. The Israelite tribes which first gained a foothold about 1225 B.C. in Palestine were nomadic. Their functional god, Jahweh, expressed the values that were foremost in their way of life. He was their champion in war and the source of the fertility of their flocks. When the Israelites conquered the Canaanites and settled upon the land, they learned from the latter the arts of agriculture. The functional gods of the Canaanites were the Baals—one for each city-state—whose business it was to give bountiful increase of fields and vineyards. It was inevitable that in taking over the skills of the soil the Jews should take over the rites that went with them.

Thus in time of war the Israelites tended to rely upon Jahweh, and in time of peace upon Baal. In addition to these there was a multitude of household deities, such as the deity of maternity. Against this fragmentation, as well as against the recognition on the part of the Israelites of the functional status of foreign gods, the prophets inveighed during the years 750–450 B.C. It was Jahweh who triumphed, but he was a new Jahweh, a god of goodness and justice who united and thereby transformed and purified the values expressed by his predecessors and the new values injected by the prophets. Jewish monotheism is not an attempt to discover either an ultimate metaphysical principle or a supreme power in the physical universe. It is the result rather of the effort to derive order out of valuational confusion. The social consciousness engendered by the prophets led to the conceiving of history as a moral order.

[3] *Isaiah* 1:15-17.

A second type of leadership—the intellectual—in the movement toward monotheism was exerted by Socrates and Plato. They influenced Christianity profoundly both directly through the Pauline-Augustinian line and indirectly through the Aristotelian-Thomistic line. The charge against Socrates that he was guilty of rejecting the traditional gods must have been justified, for in place of the Greek pantheon he and Plato offered the Greeks a universal god. It would have been inconceivable for Plato to accept the partial, limited, and mutally exclusive values symbolized by the Greek pantheon of gods, because for him there existed in the mind of God the Idea of the Good into which fitted, as a complete and harmonious whole, the pure, disembodied forms of absolute truth, beauty, and goodness.

The development of monotheism is an implicit recognition of the categorical imperative. No matter to what degree Jahweh ruled supreme over Israel, if his people did not feel that his sovereignty extended to other peoples as well, he could be no more than a functional god. He would reflect the limited values of the culture in which he originated. In affirming the one supreme god the prophets were demanding of the Israelites not only that they give up their own local deities but even that they refuse to recognize any validity to the claim of the peoples of another nation to have a god of their own.

Such an extension of Jahweh's sovereignty could not ethically have been made if Jahweh represented values that were in any sense limited. To insist that the partial values of Israel should become the values of Israel's neighbors would have been arrogant. Only a Jahweh who comprehended all values without representing any in particular could with justice be held to be the god of all peoples. This is why it took the internationalizing of Jahweh, not merely his elevation to supremacy in Israel, to make him more than a functional god. From a sociological standpoint an essential characteristic of a truly monotheistic god is his embodiment of an infinity of value.

This is what the categorical imperative implicitly recognizes. It is the practical assertion of what is symbolized by god's infinite goodness. No accident, but rather the implicit result of a logical connection, is the fact that the emergence of monotheism the world over is associated with dawning recognition of the categorical imperative. The categorical imperative may not always have been stated as explicity as it was in Jesus's "Do unto others as you would have them do unto you," Confucius's "What you do not want done, do not do to others," and Zoroaster's "Whatever thou dost not approve for thyself, do not approve for anyone else." Nevertheless, where there was a tendency toward monotheism, there was also a tendency toward ethical idealism, a demand for good will among men and for social justice—demands that imply the categorical imperative.

The Differentiation of Value

A religion may be closest to monotheism in actual practice at the point where as an organization it consists only of the small circle of disciples gathered about the founding prophet. The composite picture of god experienced by the religion's handful of devotees may, in the degree that these men can universalize their consciousness of value, be the vision of the one god. But as the brotherhood grows and spreads over the land and to other lands, the vision of the increasing multitudes of devotees with their varied interests more and more resolves into a number of separate pictures representing the various values of the various subgroups within the brotherhood.[4]

Although the devotee continues to affirm loyalty to the monotheistic god, there is implicit in his actual behavior and attitudes the assumption, more or less unconscious, that this god supports partial and finite values—those which form the conscious or unconscious value pattern of the devotee. The nominally universal god becomes in fact merely functional.

[4] Joachim Wach, *Sociology of Religion*, pp. 133-287, has brought together a great deal of the historical and sociological material which shows how religions, including the monotheistic religions, tend to begin as small groups sharing a common interest and then, as the number of devotees grows, to differentiate into numerous groups according to special interests.

Thus it is that the god of the American Negro is one who expresses the Negro's deep yearning to be free of oppression and trouble;[5] the god of the upper socioeconomic classes, including the clergy, of Southern cotton-mill towns defends the paternalistic economic pattern that prevails there;[6] the god of the bourgeoisie of America's Middletown[7] becomes beneath the official raiment of the Christian monotheistic god, the god of Culture and Progress; and the nominally Christian god of the European peasant is still in considerable degree the god of agricultural paganism—the god of fertility, vegetation, sun, and rain.[8] In some cases, as in that of the European peasant and of Mahayana Buddhism, ancient and primitive forms of worship remain much in evidence, with the new forms superimposed upon them. In other cases, notably that of Middletown's bourgeoisie, a new cult of stereotyped middle-class manners, attitudes, and beliefs associates itself with the official Christian cult and by contagion takes on the latter's sanctity.

The Roman Catholic exemplifies in his behavior the first of these two types of cases. The worship of the Catholic laity is so much directed toward special and local deities that Santayana describes it as the "pagan Christianity."[9] In some Catholic countries every worshiper has his patron, every village its saint. While god may be the formal object of worship, it is when kneeling before his saint that the Catholic may feel in most intimate contact with divinity. Here he is in the presence of a heavenly being who is personally acquainted with and concerned about his troubles, problem, and needs—in short a being who embodies the devotee's own finite life values.

The values embodied in such quasi deities may not be explicit.

[5] E. T. Kreuger, "Negro Religious Expression," *American Journal of Sociology,* XXXVIII (1932-1933), pp. 22-31.

[6] Liston Pope, *Millhands and Preachers,* pp. xvi-369.

[7] Robert S. Lynd and Helen Merrell Lynd, *Middletown in Transition* (New York: Harcourt, Brace and Company, 1937, pp. 317-318).

[8] Pitirim Sorokin, Carle C. Zimmerman, and Charles J. Galpin, editors, *A Systematic Source Book in Rural Sociology,* II (Minneapolis: University of Minnesota Press, 1931, pp. 358-361).

[9] George Santayana, *Reason in Religion,* p. 108.

But for the worshiper, his values and his patron saint have been associated from his earliest remembrance.[10] The patron saint shares in the joys and the suffering of the child's immediate social circle—parents and family. Later the devotee shares in the vicissitudes of the village and participates in the accompanying appeals to the mercy and benevolence of the local divinities. The values of his group become associated with the special and local patrons, which become for him the original and for practical purposes the ultimate gods.[11]

The Example of Calvinistic Protestantism

The rise of Protestantism in the sixteenth and seventeenth centuries, because of its association with the developing spirit of capitalism,[12] is a notable example of the unconscious transformation in practice of a nominally universal god to a functional god. The leaders of the Reformation were in protest, among other things, against the seeming prostration of the Catholic hierarchy before the idols of wealth and power. Catholicism, following the tradition of its Prophetic, Platonic, and Aristotelian ancestry, was officially opposed to the making of money through trade, business, and finance. Deeply implicated politically and economically in the feudal system, the Church had more to gain materially by continuing the classical distinction in favor of the "natural" economy based on the production of the land and against the "unnatural"[13] economy of business in which money, not production, makes wealth.

The founders of Protestantism were revolted by the spectacle of the Church despite these doctrines engaged in corrupt and usurious

[10] *Ibid.*, pp. 100-105.

[11] F. S. C. Northrop, *The Meeting of East and West*, pp. 15-65, has described and analyzed the paganism of Catholicism as practiced in Mexico, where it includes elements not only of European but also of Mayan, Aztec, Toltec, and other forms of American Indian paganism.

[12] This association has been analyzed by R. H. Tawney, *Religion and the Rise of Capitalism*, and by Max Weber, *The Protestant Ethic and the Spirit of Capitalism.*

[13] The terms are Aristotle's. *Nicomachean Ethics*, I:9.

financial activities aimed at the creation and maintenance of wealth and power. Calvinism recognized the social usefulness of commercial activities and insisted that they be conducted not only openly but also morally. Calvinism's position was that commerce had an indispensable role to play in an emerging new economic era, and ought to be conducted according to the principles of Christian morality.

This helped give Protestantism a sense of destiny. The Protestants were experiencing a Call from God. The Puritan used the doctrine of vocation to give his economic activities divine sanction. There were both a spiritual and a temporal Calling which became one. To have faith in God and to seek him was the first duty of the Christian. But the way to seek him was to labor in the affairs of practical life. "If God show you a way in which you may lawfully get more than in another way (without wrong to your soul or to any other)," wrote Richard Baxter, "if you refuse this, and choose the less gainful way, you cross one of the ends of your Calling, and you refuse to be God's steward."[14]

The combination of religious sanction and socioeconomic forces produced the peculiar Puritan-capitalist ethos. Weber terms it "worldly asceticism." It was characterized by frugality, thrift, individualism, a sense of responsibility, and iron discipline in the ordering of one's life so as best to pursue one's Calling.

This was a way of life which was to make a great contribution to the growth of modern liberalism. Its emphasis upon the freedom and responsibility of the sovereign individual became the cornerstone of the liberal conception of democracy.[15]

Yet this same individualism included a devil-take-the-hindmost spirit which was peculiarly in harmony with the conduct of competitive business enterprise. This spirit found religious sanction in the doctrine of predestination, more rigidly interpreted in Calvinism than in Catholicism. Since God has already selected the elect, the pursuit of one's Calling is not a road to salvation. It is proof,

[14] Quoted by Tawney, *op. cit.*, pp. 242-243.

[15] Ralph Barton Perry, in *Puritanism and Democracy*, and Rufus Jones, in *Mysticism and Democracy*, have shown some of the extent of the Puritan contribution to democracy.

rather that one *is* of the elect. Failure to prosper is prima facie evidence that one is not elected and called. There is no need to help others nor any reason for expecting the help of others, for salvation is predetermined for some and not for others. If the less fortunate fall by the wayside, it is due to their own "drunkenness and folly." The poor, obviously not of the elect, cannot be expected to discipline themselves. Low wages are a moral necessity to keep the poor from becoming dissolute, for only a hard life can provide the discipline they apparently cannot muster themselves. Poor relief should consist of being sent to prison at hard labor.

Here, then, was a religiously sanctioned ethos embodying the values of one socioeconomic class. In deviating from the organicism of Catholic morality, Puritanism created something new that of its day stimulated and enriched the world. Yet the new morality of individualism had at least the overtones of a class morality.

The Puritan God was not a partial god in a theological sense. The Puritans never thought him to be less than universally sovereign nor to be inclusive of less than universal value. Furthermore the useful Puritan virtues were universalized by being thought of as duties all men owe to God.

But sociologically the Puritan God was partial in that, however unconsciously, he was made to support the values of a socioeconomic class. The attempt to universalize a special ethos demonstrated, not a movement toward valuational integration, which keeps incorporating new values into itself, but rather a tendency to take the partial as final and complete. This was a different kind of partiality from that exemplified in the Catholic patrons, where partiality was recognized as such. Puritan partiality did not recognize its own finitude.

Integration and Differentiation in Evolving Valuational Coherence

It appears, then, that there are two seemingly contrary tendencies in man's religious nature. These are a movement toward valuational coherence and universality on the one hand, and toward valuational partiality or one-sidedness on the other. Yet further reflection upon the nature and significance of these two movements shows that however much they may seem to oppose one another they are really two aspects of a single movement. They are necessary to each other and to the larger process of which they are a part and within which they are a division of labor. They are essential and mutually contributive phases of valuation.

The movement toward more inclusive values presupposes the existence of limited values. The latter are experienced in acts the meaning of which are taken by the experiencer to be more or less self-evident and complete in themselves. Further doing, suffering, enjoying, and reflection reveal how the values appearing in one act are related to those of other acts. The movement toward coherence in valuation is one in which the individual re-evaluates experienced value claims in terms of the way they relate to the production of other values. A value claim is judged both by the consequences to which it leads and by the pain or joy involved in the intermediate steps which must be taken in order to realize it.

Since valuation is an active, experimental process in which a value claim is brought into coherent relation with other values or claims, the original value claim becomes reconstructed. It is modified so that it no longer does violence to but rather contributes to the other values involved. The movement toward coherence is accompanied by the refinement and purification of the values involved. This is why, from beginnings that are scarcely more than mere liking and disliking at an animal level, man can emerge with value concepts that approach the sublime.

But a consequence of the fact that valuation is active and experimental is that no value is ever finally determined. A value is definable in terms of what happens when certain actions are performed. The continual revaluation of values brings an extension and refinement of their definition. Nearly every new performance of a given kind of act is capable of adding a new qualifying phrase to the original definition of that kind of act.

This is why in valuation there are simultaneous integration and differentiation. Acts serve to show the connections that make the integration of partial values possible. But every new act creates a new value—a new claim not yet integrated with the established value structure and still standing outside it. Every act produces a challenge to the existing universe of value. At any given moment there exist both the groundwork of established value and a periphery of innumerable newly created value claims. Every thoughtful act serves to stabilize the ground by bringing ground and periphery together, but simultaneously it creates a new claim to add to the periphery.

Thus the division of labor between integration and differentiation in valuation becomes apparent. On the one hand differentiation is the aspect in which the new, the seminal, the exploratory, is created. Value claims come into existence which serve to challenge, enrich, and fertilize the old. On the other hand integration is the aspect of valuation that keeps demanding of new claims that they cease being fragmentary and partial. It is the phase that establishes the stable ground that brings the deepest, richest, most universal, and lasting satisfactions, but which at the same time provides the stepping-off place to new and challenging values.

Monotheism and the practical polytheism of the multitudes are as indispensable to one another as the legs of a stool. The one is a movement toward unity; the other a movement toward differentiation and fertilization. Life, being active, keeps moving from the base of its established values to the creation of new values, but as these differentiate there is a need felt to bring them back into the main structure. Yet the main structure grows by no mere process of accretion; coherence requires modification of both the old and the new to make them harmonize with one another in a new whole.

Great as is the achievement represented by the world-wide flowering of monotheism, it acquires part of its importance from the differentiation of values which accompanies it. Each town and borough throughout the land develops uniquenesses which contribute to the culture; society develops and improves through the contributions made to it by innumerable groups of men who meet together to pursue special interests. It would be impossible, for example, to know all the contributions to culture made by the values symbolized in the innumerable local patron saints of Catholic countries. We scarcely know in what numerous ways the values symbolized by the partial gods of the American Negro have enriched the folkways, art, and even the scientific and intellectual life of America.

We do know that the Calvinists challenged the world with new values that enriched life immeasurably. They encouraged an individualism, which, when it now needs revaluation and reconstruction to make it coherent with other values, nevertheless has contributed much both to the realization of democracy in fact and to the construction of the democratic ideal. They helped further industrial and technological growth—a contribution to the world that has been not only material but also spiritual insofar as it has brought a new vision of what we may some day have by way of abundance and well-being for all. If the bourgeois gods, in their partiality, have also been inadequate gods and have brought some of our worst evils, this is evidence, not of the undesirability of differentiation, but of the need and challenge it creates for reintegration.

CHAPTER IV

The Creative Social Act

Shall We Worship Finite Values or the Infinite Production of Values?

We are everywhere confronted by the paradox of monotheism and what amounts to polytheism existing side by side within a single religious faith.

If we analyze this paradox psychologically and sociologically, we are able to understand the process by which man develops his basic life values and gives his complete loyalty to them. We can, moreover, see the rationale of this process and thereby gain better control over it.

Human desires and acts are the basis of all valuation. Value claims, first experienced and enjoyed as consequences of acts, are tested, consolidated, and integrated as further acts reveal the cause-and-effect connections by which values are related to one another. But acts, in addition to revealing connections which make consolidation possible, have consequences which may become new value claims.

Human acts have, then, both an integrating and a differentiating effect upon values.

The integrating effect of acts results from their demonstrating the relations which make possible the reorganization of values to obtain coherence. From this there develops a value structure which guides all further acts. The value structure is the product of innumerable human acts—it is the distillation of human experience.

The differentiating effect of acts results from their production of consequences which may be prized and yet differ in small or great degree from the existing value structure. Any human act, even though guided by the existing value structure, may challenge the structure—produce new claims which may be built into the old structure as part of a reorganization.

The value structure, then, is never complete; is always evolving and growing. What we have is an evolving valuational coherence with simultaneous integration and differentiation. Integration creates the value structure to which we give our loyalties and upon which we pin our faith, while differentiation stimulates and fertilizes.

Here we encounter the great paradox in the valuational maturing of man. He must dedicate himself *both* to the finite and the infinite.

He must dedicate himself to the realization of a finite set of values which are the product of experience, historical and individual. These values constitute the working ideals to which he is committed. Yet they are finite, partial values just because they are the product of experience and because experience is always incomplete, unfinished, as long as there are men still living and experiencing.

Consequently man must also dedicate himself to the progressive reconstruction of his values. Of all the ideals to which he should be loyal, the ideal of willingness continually and objectively to reexamine values in the light of ongoing experience and rigorously to make the necessary changes has a unique status. Man commits himself, not just to a set of ideals, but to the ideal of finding more adequate ideals. Just *what* ideals remains an open question, to be settled as experience shows.

Here is the paradox. Man is called upon to be loyal to the infinite potentialities of evolving valuational coherence. Irrevocable commitment to any one set of finite values is a desecration of the ideal of infinite reconstructibility and potentiality. Yet man does live in time, and at any given moment has to be committed to a set of finite working ideals. To lack commitments is a desecration of the ideal of having ideals.

It is the genius of the religious consciousness that it has recognized this paradox and has shown the way toward its resolution. The best example is found in Christianity. The Christian God expresses in the symbolic mode the fact of the finite yet infinite nature of value. His dual nature is expressed in the great paradoxes that characterize Christianity.[1] The Christ-God is in history yet transcends it; man is finite yet self-transcendent; the kingdom of God is on earth yet not on earth; man inevitably sins yet is responsible for his sins; God is one yet a trinity, transcendent yet immanent, divine yet human.

An approach to the understanding of these paradoxes can be made by comparing the relative status of God and man. Located as he is in space and time, man does not and cannot see the full implications of his acts. The repercussions of every act inevitably and irrevocably spread through contemporary society and through history in a way no man can foresee or follow. Even the most experienced, astute, and enlightened men see only the circle of events which is relatively close to them.

God, in contrast, stands outside space and time. Not only is all the universe spread before him, but so too is all history, future as well as past. It is from the God's-eye view alone, then, that the complete and ultimate meaning of the individual acts of men can be seen. Instantaneously God views the whole of history and the fate of the repercussions of a given act.

The Christian message is that man must forever seek to know God but that he can never know him completely. To pretend to know him completely is to pretend, even while standing in time, to a God's-eye view of the universe—in short, to pretend to be God.

On this analysis the meaning of the Christian definition of

[1] These paradoxes have been described and analyzed by Reinhold Niebuhr in *The Nature and Destiny of Man.*

original sin can be understood. To play God, to be deluded into thinking one *is* God, is the sin of sins—the original sin. This is the meaning of the story of Adam and Eve, who tried to partake of forbidden knowledge, and it is the meaning that Christian thinkers from Augustine to Reinhold Niebuhr have given this doctrine. The Christian emphasis upon original sin is a way of saying that while man *must* recognize his limitations, he seldom if ever does. History is a long chronicle of men and groups who believed they had found the final word, the complete answers, the absolute truth.

In naturalistic language, we need infinitely to reconstruct experience in our quest for a better life, even while we act on present commitments. In Christian language, we need to live according to our best beliefs as to goodness and morality, but to act with the modesty and humility born of recognition that from the standpoint of eternity those beliefs are partial and incomplete.

Christianity in its wisest interpretation is perhaps the most dramatic and awesome statement ever made bringing attention to the fact that man can expect to find no final answers and must continue to reconstruct his values infinitely. In attempting final judgment upon his own works, man presumes to be God in the judgment seat. He presumes from his tiny view of history to enunciate its final meaning. This is sin in its definitive form; and the wages of sin are death, as our present civilization, with its various forms of pride, self-righteousness, and authoritarianism, seems on the verge of demonstrating.

Christianity avoids both absolutism and subjective relativism in valuation by putting the many and the particular into dialectical relationship with the one and the universal in such a way that both are parts of an evolving core of meaning. On the one hand the absolutism of final judgments by men is avoided, yet on the other hand acts are held to be susceptible to judgment. No act is sufficient to itself; there are no moral anarchy and nihilism. Differences between good and evil, right and wrong, beauty and ugliness, truth and falsity, still obtain; and tentative judgments can be made about them in the light of what insight into history man does have. Social justice is still to be sought; the refinement and enrichment of life are still ideals. God demands of man that he seek on earth the Kingdom of God; the only stricture is that man must never pretend to have found it. From a Christian standpoint democracy is the only possible ideal society for men because it is the only one that insists on its own reconstructibility.

THE NATURE OF THE CREATIVE SOCIAL ACT

There is profound insight expressed symbolically in the belief that God is the Creator. Man is here worshiping nothing less than the principle of creativity itself, rather than the limited and partial values which are produced by creativity. Here is recognition that when men become enchanted with the worth of what they have already produced and elevate it into ultimate and eternal value, their creative powers weaken and atrophy. There is always the need to press on, to recognize that each new attainment, far from marking the end of human creativity, lifts man to a vantage point from which he can see new horizons to be explored.

What needs to be sanctified are the processes which create value, not merely the values that have thus far been experienced. These processes are embodied in what, generically, may be termed the creative social act.[2]

[2] I am indebted to Henry Nelson Wieman, *The Source of Human Good,* pp. 54-83, for stimulating some of the basic ideas involved in the concept of the creative social act. His "creative event" is similar to what I have termed the "creative social act." He defines the creative event as an objective occurrence in the cosmos in which the physical and psychic energies of nature interact to produce and reorganize good. There is an ambiguity in Wieman in that he does not clarify the relation of the psychic to the physical aspects of the creative event. He maintains that the creative event can occur regardless of the involvement therein of man; yet every description he gives of the creative event appears to assume the existence in it of psychic factors. This would seem to imply some form of panpsychism, yet Wieman's whole discourse is bent upon humanity as the focal point of whatever psychic qualities are generated by the universe.

I would say, for my part, that the participation of man or some other minded animal in the creative event is a necessary accompaniment of its having psychic quality. Nevertheless the psychic factors in the creative event are not to be assigned to man exclusively and the physical factors to nature ex-

The creative social act consists of interactions of men with one another and with nature from which emerge expanding areas of common good. Since the shared activities of men always go on in a physical, biological, and ideational environment, the objects of the environment become involved in the social acts of men and acquire social meaning too. Hence the creative social act is a co-operative event in which living men participate with one another, with the ideas and objects which constitute the culture in which they live, and with nature.

Whenever two or more men come together as equals in the pursuit of any constructive activity or occupation, we have a manifestation of the creative social act. Children at play; a man and a woman acting as partners in marriage; a group of men tilling the soil; a family in which democratic, shared activities prevail; a group around a table threshing out an idea; a teacher and her children planning and executing an activity together; a team of scientists working on a technical problem; industrialists, laborers, technicians, contributing over the decades to the development of the automobile; generations of men over a period of centuries developing the democratic tradition—all are examples of the creative social act.

The creative social act may also be manifested even in the solitary activity of a man. A man with a book, or a man alone with an idea, great or small, is interacting with something that has been presented by his culture. Here the social act is an interaction between a man now living and generations of men who once lived. The same is true of a man alone with nature. He brings to nature ideas, not all of his own invention, which help determine the meaning of whatever relations he has with nature. Even the "man with the hoe," or the woodsman with an ax, however lacking in ideas he may or may not be as he carries on his special trans-

---

clusively. Instead the physical is simply one way or level in which or at which man and nature interact, and the psychic another way. Physical and psychic are not different in kind but indicate qualitatively different modes of interaction between man and nature.

action with nature, is engaged in an act which is not only productive or creative, but which is clearly social; for the implement he uses is a cultural implement, and that which he produces has social consequences.

When values emerge in the creative social act, a process of reorganization is going on which generates new meanings, integrates them with the old, endows each successive act with a wider range of reference, and molds the life of man into a more deeply unified totality of meaning. The varieties, contrasts, and diversities of life are being transformed into a more inclusive whole, while at the same time there are being created a richer range and variety of new meanings. Here is evolving coherence characterized by both integration and differentiation.

The creative social act depends upon participation and communication; it consists of broadening and deepening the community. Communication is essential to the creative social act because it serves to bring together and relate the values and meanings accumulated by many lives. Communication not only brings together the experiences of men now living but also the experiences of men throughout history. Because the creative social act lives on these contributions, it is essential to its flourishing that the scope of communication and of community be constantly increased. This requires the full participation of men now living as well as the making of the culture itself available to the creative social act through its living participants. There must be more sharing of experiences and points of view than we have; individuals and groups that tend to be excluded from the community must be brought in; the barriers that separate men and their experiences must be progressively broken down.

The Transcendent Quality of the Creative Social Act

One of the most distinctive characteristics of the creative social act is that while its participants contribute purposefully to it, none can know or predict the outcome. From the situation of a man wrestling with the ideas in a book there may be outcomes unforeseen either by author or reader. From a gathering of men come together in some common cause there may emerge ways of accomplishing their end which no one had seen in the beginning. Furthermore, as new means and instruments are discovered by the group, its very goals and purposes are reconstructed.

Indeed the way—the way of all ways—to destroy the creativity of a group is for any one or more members to try to predetermine the outcome. Equality is destroyed; cooperation gives way to competition; helpfulness becomes blind following; leadership becomes domination bent on preserving its own vested interest rather than in releasing creativity. Here is original sin in definitive form operating to destroy creativity—the Creator—itself.

In creative social acts there develops a group spirit which is the invention of no one person and which is larger than any one person. In fact, it is greater than the combined participants, if the latter are taken merely additively. The group spirit has qualities which cannot be fully accounted for by the combined individual personal qualities of the participants. Somehow, in ways unknown even to them, they develop a morale and an *esprit de corps* which help determine the outcome of the common effort.

The creative social act generates qualities which transcend those of its contributing factors. The communication and participation which characterize the social act generate a spirit which seizes the individual men involved and transforms them. They enter the social act to contribute their finite and particular values, and are so caught up in the power of the process they help produce that they undergo radical transformation of outlook and personality. There is produced in them a wider and deeper vision.

The creative social act produces what man in his finiteness does not intend. Devotion to the social act is not mere humanism in the usual sense; the social act cannot be used to shape the world closer to a set of finite ideals because it works in such a way as to change the ideals themselves. The social act achieves outcomes which the men involved cannot predict; hence it is more than merely human. Yet the social act is transcendent, not in the sense of being beyond or outside the temporal and spatial world. It is a new and overpowering quality that is generated by the interaction of energies in the world.

The creative social act is an objective event in the world, to which man makes his contribution. Without being supernatural, it is superhuman in several respects.

For one thing, the creative social act is a product of the cosmos, of which man is but a part. Man's body and brain are organizations of natural energy. Nature, not he, produced them. His use of them is subject to the conditions imposed by nature. Furthermore, the human participants in the creative social act deal with natural objects and forces as part of the process of dealing with one another. There is the soil to be tilled; the sun, rain, and wind to be utilized or adapted to; the rivers to be dealt with; the electromagnetic energy of the universe loosed and in some small measure controlled. Man is involved for better or worse with nothing less than the movements of the universe itself. Creative social acts emerge within the vast ferment of the cosmos. It is appropriate that man approach the creative social act in the spirit of hopeful humility, with a profound sense of dependence upon the forces that generated him and with which he must work in trying to shape his destiny.

The creative social act is superhuman in another sense. The social act generates qualities which transcend those of its contributing factors and which transform existence and life. When men give of themselves freely to the social act, ideas are created and acts accomplished which stun their imaginations. They are swept away in the group spirit that develops. New horizons appear, and the personality of each participant is lifted up and changed. The good participant—the one who is neither rigid nor herd-minded—is the one who is able to surrender to this spirit and to let it transform him, even while he does not lose his distinctive individuality. There emerges a new self capable of more distinctive contributions to the common effort.

There is profound truth in the religious conviction that "Except a man be born again, he cannot see the kingdom of God."

CHAPTER V

The Valuational Mode: Education

The Religious Task of the School

RELIGIOUS quality in the behavior, character, and experience of children can develop through their participation in creative social activity. Through participation the child can discover for himself how the creative social act produces and increases value. He learns to place his faith in the social act as the source of value, not because he has been exhorted to, but because he actually experiences its productivity. He finds that voluntary cooperative activity creates more good both for himself and others than does coerced activity, which breeds reluctance and antagonism. He discovers through experience that good human relations create more good—that to weaken them by egotistic acts weakens creativity.

Ability to cultivate and promote the creative social act is a primary religious art and skill learned through participation. Participation develops a whole range of social and creative abilities. The child learns to live, work, and play with others in ways which maximize the good experienced. As he becomes more skillful and confident, he enters into creative social activities more freely.

Participation in the creative social act helps the child continuously build and rebuild a structure of ideal value to which he commits his life. The child brings his value claims to the creative social act. There they interact with the claims of other children and the claims of society as represented by the teacher, as the group plans and executes whatever practical activity it is concerned with. Within the activities of the group a dual process of valuational integration and differentiation takes place. As values integrate and are enriched by newly differentiated values, the child forms new and deeper allegiances.

The religious task of the school, then, is the double one of promoting the creative social act and of helping the child develop a growing set of ideals by which to live. Each of these tasks needs to be considered in greater detail.

The Creative Social Act in the School

The creative social act is capable of becoming the characteristic feature of the life of the school. It can become the typical context within which most of the teaching and learning in the school go on. Teachers and students alike can be regarded as potential participants in the social act. They can contribute to learning by contributing first of all to the social act.

Teachers and students can cooperatively plan and carry out most of the educative activities of the school. They can together decide upon the outcomes to be desired, plan how to achieve these outcomes, organize a cooperative attack upon the problem, and evaluate actual accomplishments. Every phase, from setting goals to evaluating results, from planning to the actual carrying out of the work, can involve participation on a cooperative basis. Everyone, including the teacher, can give and be encouraged to give of himself to the creative social act, so that the group can realize as much value as possible.

On this basis the curriculum would turn out to be essentially a continuous process of cooperative problem-solving. The expressions "problem-solving" and "cooperative" indicate two essential features of the creative social act.

Problem-solving is essential because no process can be creative when its outcome is predetermined or known in advance. Any creative act is an exploration, a pushing into unknown territory, with the outcome always in doubt and sometimes very different from what had been hoped or expected. Since the outcome is unknown, a creative act is necessarily accompanied by feelings of doubt. The presence or absence of such feelings is the test of whether a given situation is problematic or not.

If the curriculum were put on a problem-solving basis, it would consist of a series of inquiries and investigations, with one problem leading to another and with minor problems rising within the contexts of larger problems or accumulating to form major problems. This would be, even from the standpoint of the psychology of learning, sounder educational practice than much of what prevails today, because investigating, exploring, discovery, are the characteristic modes in which learning occurs.

Exploratory activity is one of the most striking characteristics of the very young child and can be encouraged and guided by the mature participants in the creative social act. As the child matures he can through experience gain familiarity with and control of more sophisticated and systematic methods and techniques of investigation.

Not that problem-solving is a merely scientific undertaking. Scientific quality is but one of problem-solving's many characteristics. Artistic production, for example, has the elements of doubt, perplexity, and trying out which characterize all creative activity. Artistic production is an attack upon a problem. But the problem-solving involved in artistic production has in many ways a different qualitative "feel" from problem-solving that is more scientific. Scientific problem-solving requires creative organization of facts and ideas, whereas artistic problem-solving requires the creative organization of feelings and emotions. The problem of achieving good human relations is another example of problem-solving at other than a strictly scientific level. But whether the content of a creative act is in the domain of art, natural science, social science, human relations, or elsewhere, the approach is in the spirit of experimental inquiry.

But to be creative, problem-solving should be a cooperative undertaking. When a variety of participants stimulate one another by contributing their individually unique backgrounds and approaches, they generate a creative spirit. To accomplish this, each individual needs to have a share in determining the purposes of the group. This enables him to accept these purposes as his own. He becomes a part of the group and can work with it in accomplishing the goal held in common. The existence of a common goal is what holds the members together in cooperative relationship to one another.

It is true, however, both in school life and in the occupations of men everywhere that individuals need opportunity to withdraw temporarily from group activity to work individually. The individual can seldom be fully productive unless he has a degree of privacy. But the point is that individual activity should be within the context of group activity—should grow from or be contributory to the experience of the group.

A child, or any adult creative artist or thinker for that matter, needs to withdraw to consult his own feelings and ideas in order to produce something satisfying to himself and others. But any work of art, whether it be in the realm of the fine arts, useful arts, or ideas, expresses or communicates something. From the perspective of childhood, every accomplishment, every object constructed from physical materials, every idea built from childhood experiences, every newly acquired skill, is a work of art. To be worthy in the eyes of its maker it must be potentially contributable to someone. The child's own school group, aside from his own immediate family, is the most likely "someone" to whom he may contribute his "works of art" and by whom his accomplishments may be recognized. His accomplishments are more likely to be acceptable if they either form part of an already ongoing cooperative activity or else are used as a fresh stimulant to new directions in cooperative activity or shared experience. Few things are so disturbing as repeatedly to attempt contributions which make no apparent difference to pursuits the group is carrying on, and which win at best only polite and perfunctory attention from a group impatient to proceed with other things.

An Example

The following is illustrative of the way work can be conducted in a school where the creative social act is recognized as the backbone of the curriculum. Cooperative problem-solving is the basic method of teaching and learning used by the teacher and the children in this example:

The weather had been unusual for a number of days. There had been rains of almost cloudburst proportions, extreme humidity, and chillness not common at that time of year.

The members of the eighth-year group were conducting their usual early-morning news discussion. The subject of the unusual weather came up, and Miss Cohen encouraged the children to talk about their personal experiences of the past few days. Bob's yard had been flooded, Mary had been riding with her father when he had to stop the car because of the downpour, Katherine had . . .

The discussion turned to the question of what could have caused such unusual weather. Soon the children were citing other kinds of weather they had experienced and were making suggestions about possible causes. Many were challenging the adequacy of each other's suggestions.

The discussion ended at such a peak of unsatisfied curiosity that Miss Cohen and the children decided that they would pursue the matter further the next day.

The next morning the group systematically organized on the blackboard the questions raised the day before and decided to investigate them.

The questions were divided among a number of research committees, each composed of three or four children. During the succeeding days each committee planned and carried through an attack upon its particular problems.

The work of the committee on What Causes Rain? was typical. The rain committee visited the library and gathered all the books, pamphlets, and charts containing material on its topic that it could find. It then spent two or three hours in the classroom, on successive days, sitting around a table reading, discussing, and planning.

Arthur, after being absorbed in a book for half an hour or so, would turn to George, who had been similarly occupied, to compare notes. Perhaps one would help the other interpret what he had read, or both would recall experiences related to the material in question, or a plan for some further action would take nebulous shape.

The committee reached the point where it felt it had some definite answers to its problems. It invited Miss Cohen to sit with it for a few minutes to discuss its findings and to consider how it might proceed further. After Miss Cohen left, the committee continued its planning. It was decided that Arthur and George would try to work out a plan for distilling some water, in order to illustrate both evaporation and condensation; and that Mary and Bob would work out a large chart, visible the length of the room and painted in poster colors, portraying the water cycle.

Meanwhile other committees were pursuing their own activities. One made arrangements for the class to visit the local weather bureau. After making a pilot excursion itself to the bureau, this committee made a presentation to the class to orient the latter for the excursion, and made all arrangements for the excursion. Another committee made a set of hand-drawn lantern slides which showed the behavior of high- and low-pressure areas. Another group experimented with prisms and with glycerine-coated water drops in order to understand the causes of rainbows.

There was a planning committee which had been set up by the class to coordinate the activities of the various committees. One of the most important functions of this committee was to schedule periods two or three times each week during which committees would make progress reports to the class. It was during these periods that the rain committee demonstrated distillation and explained its water-cycle chart, the high-and-low-pressure-area committee projected its lantern slides and explained them to the class, the rainbow committee demonstrated with its prisms and water drops, and the weather-bureau committee planned the excursion with the class.

Each progress report created the occasion for general critical discussion, evaluation of progress, and further planning. The most important outcome of these discussions was the class's decision that it wanted to plan and set up its own weather bureau.

The weather-bureau project started before the research committees had completed their work. In planning the weather bureau, the class decided that it would need a barometer, an anemometer, a thermometer, a wet- and dry-bulb thermometer, a rain gauge, and a weather vane. The class felt it would be more fun and more worth-while if these instruments should be built by the children themselves, even though some, like the thermometer, could be readily purchased.

Six construction committees were appointed, one for each instrument. Every child in the class served on a construction committee as well as on one of the original research committees.

The work of the anemometer committee, though somewhat more complex than that of most of the other committees, illustrates the kind of experiences most of the construction committees had.

The anemometer committee, after looking into some books, drew a plan of its project. The four cups to catch the wind were to be halves of two tennis balls. The large gear from a discarded eggbeater was to be used to "gear down" the revolutions of the cups so that each revolution could be counted. The finished anemometer was to be calibrated by mounting it on a car and cruising at 5, 10, 15, 20, and 25 miles an hour, counting revolutions. One child arranged with his father to help with this, using the family car after school hours.

When all six instruments were finished, the children started taking daily observations and recording them on large charts visible throughout the room. Each morning there was a discussion of the significance of the readings, in terms of what had been learned about the behavior of weather through the research committees. Daily weather reports were sent to the other classes in the school.

The class derived a great deal of satisfaction from its school weather bureau, the successful operation of which served as a culmination to their weeks of research and construction.

The outcome of this activity was predetermined by no one. The teacher stimulated, guided, helped the group organize and direct its energies, and undoubtedly had in mind definite values she hoped would be realized. Yet there was no way for her to know in advance just what would result from the interaction of her efforts with the contributions of the children. Group, not individual, decisions determined policy. Neither the individual nor the merely aggregate wills of the participants could have produced what happened. Rather, interstimulation generated one new development after another which by reflexive action continuously restimulated the participants. The teacher gave of and yet submitted herself and her ideas to the creative social act and helped the children do the same. They let the creative social act be the final determiner of what happened.

The children not only were acquiring in a functional way a great amount of knowledge and understanding related to weather, but, what is even more important, they were learning to be effective participants in the creative social act. It is not possible in the written report to record the innumerable incidents showing this—the clash of individual desires and wills and the settling of these in ways that best promoted the creative process; the drawing out and encouragement of the shy and withdrawn; the slow realization by the overaggressive and the domineering personalities of their deleterious effect upon the joint effort, and their experiments in finding more acceptable ways of contributing; the gradual relaxing of the socially awkward; the struggle with and the growth of facility in the process of planning.

Were it possible to record such material, one significant fact would stand out. This is that social and methodological skill develops in the children not solely as a result of the teacher's constant help and guidance. The children are the teachers of one another. For example, when a group of children is involved in an activity which it regards as its own, the effectiveness with which it will deal with the disruptive participant is superior to that of many teachers. Undesirable modes of participation bring a quick response from the majority, who place social pressure upon the offender. The offender learns from such experiences that if he is to be accepted he must be more acceptable—that he must find more desirable ways of entering into and participating in activities. Usually he begins to experiment at finding such ways. Even more than helping the children learn social skills, the teacher's task is to help them learn to help one another develop these skills. He can for example, in the midst of the children's work, help them become sensitive to the symptoms displayed by the attention-seeker or by the too-easily stimulated personality, and he can help them devise tactics for dealing with such cases.

Implicit in the above record of the children's activities is their developing sense of values and their growing loyalty to the ideal values emerging in their experience. By living and working together, by finding scientifically effective ways of approaching problems, they are formulating democratic and methodological ideals and living according to them. This is made more explicit in the following section, in which is included an example of growing loyalty to one of these ideals—the scientific method.

The Scientific Quality in the Creative Social Act

The creative processes productive of good have a scientific as well as a social aspect. The values accepted, the policies set, the decisions made within the context of the creative social act, can be determined by methods of judgment which have the experimental quality commonly recognized as characterizing scientific investigation. Children can be helped to learn to base their choices upon prediction of probable outcomes as indicated by previous experience. As they attempt to make judgments about what should be done in given situations, they can be helped to form the habit of first finding out what can be done. They can be helped to base choices realistically upon investigation of existing possibilities and resources, and to take into account limiting circumstances and factors. Children can form habits of seeking evidence for their beliefs, of trying out and testing ideas before accepting them.

Above all, they can be helped to see that it is the obligation of everyone proposing a truth claim to indicate the methods by which the claim was arrived at and the evidence in its support. Questions such as "Who said so?" and "How does he know?" can become second nature to children whose experiences have been guided in such a way that they have seen the fallibility of human judgment and the precautions that must be taken to insure validity. If questions are raised by those guiding the children as to the reliability of the authority on which statements are made in books, by adults, by the children themselves, the children can become sensitive to the signs which indicate reliability in various areas and to the signs which throw suspicion upon claims to authority.

It is good to know the truth, but is is even better, in the long run, to master the methods of inquiry by which truth becomes known. Which shall it be—loyalty to a given claim to truth, a given doctrine or belief, or loyalty to the methods which establish and certify to the validity of such claims? The choice is between an absolutistic and an experimental approach to life; it is nothing less, in fact, than a choice between submission to original sin and loyalty to creativity.

In the following example, from a science notebook written by a seventh-grade girl, the child's growing devotion to ideals of scientific procedure can be seen. Her project happened to involve scientific subject matter—the study of aquaria and their care. But the subject matter could just as well have dealt with human relations, aesthetic material, or anything else. Not the subject matter involved, but loyalty to the kind of processes which result in valid judgments is what made the quality of this girl's experience scientific.

One day the children were having an argument about the amount of air needed by the fish in our aquaria. Tommy said that each fish needed one gallon of water to have enough air, but some other students disagreed with Tommy's rule.

I decided to find out who was right, so I looked in some books. I found one book which said there should be 240 square inches of water surface for every inch of fish. But I found another book which said only 200 square inches were needed.

I asked Mr. Brandt about it. He said maybe Clara and I could experiment to see which book was right.

We tried putting the same number of fish in aquaria of different sizes. We watched to see which aquarium had fish that came to the top for air. When we found the smallest aquarium in which the fish did not come up, we measured the fish and the aquarium. We found that the aquarium had only 150 square inches per inch of fish. We decided both books must be wrong.

We told Mr. Brandt, and he wondered if we had used different kinds of fish, the answers might have been different.

Afterwards we decided our results were only good for guppies.

This girl was learning through experience to evaluate the authority on which statements are made, to set up experiments testing claims to truth, to limit her conclusions by not going beyond the data. In doing this she was mastering some of the techniques of scientific discovery.

More important, she was acquiring a disposition to place her faith in objective methods of inquiry. She was learning to approach life with a readiness to explore, delve, search.

Her experiment happened to be individually conducted. But part of her teacher's responsibility was to show her that in presenting her results to her fellow students she had an obligation to make her methods of obtaining them as clear as the results themselves. Only if the other students could see and check her procedures would they be able to judge the validity of her results.

To present results while refusing to disclose how they are arrived at is the fundamental technique upon which authoritarianism depends. The authoritarian when he acts keeps his reasons a guarded secret so that they cannot be criticized. When he enunciates "truth" he refuses to disclose how he arrives at it. In contrast, the insistence that not only results but methods, not only acts but reasons, be opened to public scrutiny is the most fundamental of democratic safeguards. This insures that motives, reasons, evidence, alleged causes, may be examined, criticized, and judged. This is why the basic rule of scientific procedure is that it shall be conducted in public view. The scientist may work alone in his laboratory, but unless he publishes an account of his procedures so they can be checked and verified he cannot get his results accepted by his colleagues. This means that science, despite the solitude of the laboratory, is by its nature a social undertaking.

Here we have the basic connection between the creative social act and the scientific approach to the conduct of life. In the degree that children are helped to develop scientific quality in their various activities and experiences, they are learning to share with others in the creation of a more satisfying existence. The girl in the example was learning to place her faith in the creative social act by paying attention to its methodological aspects.

Faith in the Reconstructibility of Existence

A fundamental religious faith—faith in the potential improvability or reconstructibility of existence—can develop in a child through participation in creative activities. Faith in the reconstructibility of existence develops when the child experiences success in response to challenge. Both elements—success and challenge—are necessary. Repeated success without challenge only gives experience an insipid flavor, while repeated challenge without success only results in frustration. The net result in either case is cynicism—and cynicism, the utter lack of faith in life's potentialities, is the essence of the irreligious attitude.

The following example shows how increasing the challenge, but not to the point of danger, leads to more significantly productive performance and a more solid feeling of success.

Donald, Colin, and Ralph, sixth-graders, were attempting to construct a working model of a telegraph sounder as their contribution to a study of communication being carried on by the members of their class. They had found directions for constructing a sounder in a science book, and they had planned for and already brought from home the needed tools and materials. Despite the teacher's suggestions, they would not, before beginning construction, devote any time to reading up on the principles of magnetism and electric currents which were involved in the operation of the sounder. They had their directions for construction and did not wish to bother with principles. As they industriously worked away on their sounder, Mrs. Stevenson quietly noted several errors they were making. They were making the sounder bar of copper, whereas only iron would respond to the magnetic pull to be induced in the coils they were winding around two nails. Furthermore, they were using bare instead of insulated wire in winding their coils, not realizing that the current would "short" instead of circulating through the coils. Although this showed that the boys did not understand what they were doing, the teacher made no comment. A day or two later, when the completed instrument was hooked up and tried out, there were protests of anguish from the three boys when it failed to work.

The boys worked over their instrument for some time, becoming increasingly disturbed as they could not find the difficulty.

Mrs. Stevenson made a point of being busy elsewhere. But when she felt the boys were getting dangerously close to giving up, she casually asked them if they knew the principles of what makes a complete circuit, and what materials will respond to magnetic forces. She suggested that it might be worth finding out whether their sounder bar was made of the right material and whether their coils were constructed in such a way as to get a complete circuit.

With this, the minimum hinting that could be done consistent with adequate direction, Mrs. Stevenson left to busy herself elsewhere. The boys dug out their reference books and on the basis of considerable research into principles were able to find their error and remedy it.

In order to become convinced that life is improvable, the child needs to have many experiences in which, through his collaboration with others and with the resources of their environment, the quality of life actually is made better. The chronic feeling of insecurity does not yield to the mere resolve to be more courageous. Too many failures, too many rebuffs, are taken as proof that existence is not improvable.

But the boys in the example experienced success only after a challenge, the severity of which made success all the more satisfying. We err when we seek to direct children along a straight road to successful performance. Children, like everyone else, learn through their mistakes. We should not short-circuit their thinking and efforts by removing difficulties too soon. In this case the boys, because they had failed, willingly looked into, studied, and learned a great deal about the principles of electricity, whereas previously they had resisted all efforts to persuade them to undertake such study. But most important of all, by facing difficulties they learned the meaning of success.

The child cannot and should not be protected from all suffering, disappointment, and failure. Faith in the transformability of existence necessarily includes the consciousness of existing evil. The educational problem is not to keep the child unaware of life's pain, but to help him know its existence and, knowing it, to face it with courage and confidence.

The trouble with the school, however, is that so often it sets up conditions which militate against the child's experiencing the increase of good in life. The school is often obsessed with creating artificial barriers for children to hurdle; with placing them in a competitive relation with one another in the running of what amounts to obstacle courses; with insisting upon making tasks difficult for mere narrow disciplinary effect. The child's own present life contains enough problems and difficulties to provide all the challenge he needs. The school's problem is to get inside the child's experiences, help him identify and define his own problems, and give him the aid he needs in working them out.

Some of the worst sinning of the schools in this respect has come from the ingrained belief that a child learns best, not when he is solving his present problems, but when he is equipping himself with an arsenal of heavy artillery for attacking problems in some distant and hypothetical future. One grade in the school sequence becomes a preparation for the next grade, one level for the next level, all levels for adult life.

The best way to prepare for future life, however, is not to prepare for it at all, but to concentrate on being the most effective possible person in meeting the inherent challenges of present existence. But no: the child is asked to accept tasks for which he is not yet ready and in which he sees no value, other than the value of appeasing adults and the value of winning the prestige that comes with high performance in the things that adults praise. The net result of this approach is that only a fraction of the students in our schools find satisfaction in school work. To most it is a necessary evil, to be suffered and endured but seldom enjoyed. To be sure, the child often has been persuaded to have a blind faith that somehow this is all for the good. But the only faiths worth having are those that are based upon clear vision of the realities of existence. Unless the school can find ways to help children experience actual good during their years in school, children's faith in the improvability of existence must continue to suffer.

The child's participation in the creative social act enables him to live in the present. The problems selected through joint teacher-

and-pupil planning are real to the child. He feels their challenge, sometimes he is overwhelmed and defeated by them, but his defeats bring home to him his realization of the strength of the creative social act, provided the school can involve him in that act often enough and deeply enough for him to experience its power.

When a child has a hand in selecting the problems upon which he is to work, he does look—or if not he can be helped to look—toward the future. It is a part of intelligent conduct that the individual try to foresee as many consequences as possible while he makes his choices. The school should help the child do so. But to help the child perceive and take into account future consequences is an entirely different thing from asking him to tackle a problem whose only significance for him is that he has been told if he solves it life will be better ten years hence. The nub of the question is whether someone else is to look ahead to consequences for him, or whether he is to be expected to do his looking ahead himself, with help. Living in the present instead of living for a hypothetical future puts greater responsibility upon the child, is less arbitrary, and enables him to find the satisfactions which bolster his faith in life.

The Development of Ideal Values

Participation in the creative social act is an experience within which a structure of ideal value emerges. A cooperatively planned activity should have some objectively desirable yet subjectively hoped-for outcome. The outcome should be desired in fact, and also it should be desirable in terms of objective evaluation of its merits. The evaluation and determination of desired and desirable outcomes should be a matter for joint consideration by teachers and pupils. In such an undertaking the students and the teachers bring their respective value claims before the group for consideration, with the intention that discussion and investigation will clarify the relations among the various claims and will enable the group to agree upon outcomes which integrate as many as possible of the values involved, many of which will have to be transformed in the process.

This requires the practice and learning of a discipline—the discipline or logic of making value judgments.

Perhaps the first and most important thing to note about such a discipline is that it does not develop either through an act of "will" on the part of the youngster or in response to the direct analytical teaching of its elements. The logical disciplines involved in valuation can develop only in their actual practice. But even when this is recognized, the belief may remain that the correct practice can be induced through exhortation, reward and punishment, or direct teaching of the principles involved.

What is overlooked in such viewpoints is the fact that discipline develops internally within activity and does not enter it from without. A child who has been drawn into the creative social act finds satisfaction therein and begins consciously or unconsciously to find and practice the disciplines that seem to conserve and increase these satisfactions. The creative social act disciplines because of the satisfaction and goodness that it creates.

But even though the logical disciplines in creativity may develop unconsciously at first, there is a need to bring them into consciousness. Although they develop internally and their existence is not at first recognized in consciousness, it is possible for outside help to enter the situation and aid the child to formulate explicit principles of conduct. These must be based on what has been experienced, but what otherwise might not become consciously organized.

The conscious formulation of the rules of procedure which become evident in such situations is important for a number of reasons. For one thing their explicit statement aids their further refinement and development. To elucidate the principles involved by the generalization of actual experience is to become more conscious of their nature and of how they might be further modified. The relationship between discourse and practice is reciprocal; improved practice makes possible more refined statements of principles, and vice versa. The differentiation of behavior into a logic of discourse and a logic of operation sets into motion a spiral of growth in which each element secures leverage from the other.

For another matter, the elucidation of principles makes possible their conscious practice. It marks a change from the participation in valuation with childlike unconsciousness of what is involved to a more mature and deliberate pursuit of valuation as a science.

What, then, in addition to the initial cultivation of spontaneous creativity, can the school do to promote the growth of a consciously practiced discipline of valuation?[1]

The opportunity to help children develop a science of valuation occurs in those situations in which value judgments are actually made by them. The making of such judgments is initiated at the point where there is a disturbance in the ongoing life process of the child. When things are going smoothly, there is no occasion to investigate what would be better for the future. But when something goes wrong, then an unevaluated immediate desire for something better is felt. The disturbance of equilibrium may be caused by the stimulation of a challenging environment, by growth processes which open up new visions of things to accomplish, by some obstacle to ongoing activity, by a threat to the *status quo,* by a conflict in the life values at work, or by any one of an infinite number of other disturbing or stimulating changes in the individual-environment relationship. But in any case there is immediately and uncritically felt a desire for a different state of affairs.

These desires need to be evaluated, not by another person for the child, but by the child himself with guidance. The desires of the child may and often will appear to be poorly taken, fantastic, or even dangerous. Many of them, on the other hand, will from the start appear sound and promise fruitful consequences. But in either case they are the occasion for investigation and testing by the child.

To many it will sound unrealistic to propose that children be

[1] What follows is an application to educational theory of principles elucidated by John Dewey, *Theory of Valuation,* pp. vii-67.

expected to examine critically their own desires. But in the degree that the child actually expects to realize his desires, it is more natural for him to criticize them than not. The intention to realize a desire leads the child to examine the steps that must be taken. When he sees what is involved in achieving that which he wants, he is led to a criticism of the desire itself. Unless the steps seem to him worth taking, the desire cannot retain its hold upon him. Consequently, the question is not whether a child *will* criticize his desires; it is rather whether he gets adequate help and guidance in going about his criticism in an intelligent fashion.

Criticism of a desire consists essentially of a survey and appraisal of the things that must be done to achieve the desire. The child's attention is directed to the factors in the situation that must be taken into account; the means and materials that are at hand; the intermediate acts that must be performed.

What is important about these "next steps" is that they usually bring consequences *in addition* to the ones which, as desires, are in the forefront of consciousness. The paying of attention to these additional consequences enables the child to decide whether or not he is willing to take whatever steps are necessary. If they strike him as being good, as not conflicting with the groundwork of values he already holds, his original desire becomes justified in his mind and comes closer to achieving the status of an actual value. If, on the other hand, the intermediate steps bring consequences that conflict with his working values or are even seen to negate the original desire itself, then the desire is given up and loses claim to value status.

Usually, however, the picture is neither black nor white. What happens is that in some respects the intermediate steps seem desirable and in others not. This calls for a modification of the original desire. It can be modified in such a way that the resulting change of the necessary intermediate steps makes them and their concomitant consequences more acceptable. Thus there is a reconstruction of the desire which brings it closer to value status.

The essential nature of what is involved in the foregoing should be noted. By relating means and ends a value judgment is tentatively made. The relating of means and ends is at the heart of the science of valuation.

Assuming now that the child has modified his desire in such a way that it involves steps which bring an acceptable set of consequences, what he now has is a plan of action and an end-in-view. The plan of action consists of the intermediate steps which have been decided upon as necessary and desirable. The end-in-view consists of the entire set of consequences, including the modified desire, which are expected to result.

This points to another cardinal principle of valuation. When a desire thus changes its status to an end-in-view it not only becomes transformed, but it is brought into coherent relationship with other outcomes that are considered good. Instead of a set of unrelated desires or of desires unrelated to values previously established by experience, there appears a degree of valuational coherence. This coherence is still, however, to be tested—it is still a claim.

The next step is for the child actually to carry out the plan of action that has thus been formulated. This action has an end-in-fact, as distinguished from the end-in-view which activates it. The end-in-fact is the actual outcome of the act as distinct from the desired outcome. It is necessary for purposes of analysis to distinguish between ends-in-fact and ends-in-view because in practice the seldom exactly coincide. The end-in-view is the predicted, hoped-for outcome. But the end-in-fact is the actual outcome. The actual outcome usually, if not always, falls short of, exceeds, or is qualitatively different in some degree from what was hoped or planned.

The performance of the act constitutes the overt testing of the value claim, which at this stage of inquiry has the form of an end-in-view. The child's end-in-view predicts that certain results felt to be good will come from a specified act. The completion of the act shows whether these results *do* come; in other words it shows whether the act itself is as valuable an act as it was predicted to be. A disparity between the end-in-fact and the end-in-view presents the child with a new aspect of his effort at valuation. It calls for readjustment in which means and ends-in-view become better related to one another. Which is to be modified, the means or the end-in-view? Actually, neither can be modified without modifying the other. The end-in-view cannot be kept in its original form while the means alone are adjusted, because an adjustment of the means brings not only the desired change in expected outcomes but additional or concomitant outcomes as well. When these last are incorporated into the end-in-view, it too becomes transformed.

Consequences seldom if ever come singly. They come in groups, and their multiple nature must be taken into account in every plan to use certain means. The error of fixing upon but one consequence of an act and overlooking the conjoined consequences is the basis of the fallacy of "the end justifies the means." The end (or more properly, to employ the distinction previously made, the end-in-view) may be a good one, but if ruthless means are employed they produce ends-in-fact which destroy whatever value might have resulted.

Action, by bringing to light concomitant ends, provides the test of the value of an end-in-view. In addition it provides the factual basis for reconstructing the end-in-view so that its value is increased. This is the net result of bringing means into better relationship with ends-in-view. Following a test, new or modified means are chosen which, because they bring concomitant values, modify the end-in-view itself. Testing and reconstruction must continue indefinitely. Meanwhile the tentative nature of values does not prevent their being working guides to life.

Because situations and conditions change, because individuals grow and environments become modified, the ends-in-fact of repeated acts never remain the same and never can be fully predicted. Yet there is continuity in the changes that occur. Because there is change, ends-in-view must be continually retested; but because there is continuity, every test makes its contribution—every end-in-view is partially justified, even though it must later be modified.

As an end-in-view becomes more fully tested and more adequately reconstructed, the point at which it passes from the status of a value claim to a certified and established value can perhaps not be determined except arbitrarily. All of a child's values, being reconstructible, are in that sense but claims. Yet testing and reconstruction bring a valuational coherence which gives many of the child's values such stability that they can be accepted as a working basis for action. This is the practical test of when a value claim becomes a value.

At several points in the above analysis mention has been made of the fact that there is always a groundwork or foundation of value, in the light of which value claims are tested. To state the relationship more precisely, the selection of means to an end-in-view involves some conception of whether the concomitant outcomes are valuable or not. The question naturally arises, then, as to how these prior conceptions of value become established in the first place. They are the results of previous experiencing and valuing. In their function as ground they are taken as reasonably well established and certified in experience. They are taken for granted at the moment because the original upset in equilibrium which initiates inquiry focuses consciousness upon some other point. The desire created by the upset directs attention to some point in the established value structure which is challenged, brought before consciousness, and put on trial as a value claim. Any part of the structure may be and is challenged at any time. The part not challenged provides a base of operations and a standard of evaluation. But since the entire process consists essentially of bringing means and consequences into more harmonious relationship, every change at the focal point modifies the ground itself. This is the meaning of evolving valuational coherence.

For an illustration of some of the foregoing points, the example of the boys building a telegraph sounder, described on a previous page, may be recalled. Here, the value beginning to dawn in the consciousness of the boys was their realization of the worth of understanding basic principles whenever one is attempting to do something. But they were not aware of this value at the start.

The example shows the typical phases in the act of valuation. In this case the disturbance of equilibrium which initiated activity was the original interest in making a telegraph sounder. A value claim—the anticipated satisfaction of having a working model—came into the forefront of consciousness. But this original value claim was defined in shortsighted terms—the boys wanted to achieve satisfaction without providing time for understanding the electromagnetic principles involved.

This claim motivated the first actions of the boys, which ended in near frustration when the instrument would not work. The end-in-view or value claim was just a working model, not a working model *plus* understanding of principles. But the end-in-fact was a model that would not work. Here was a new upset in equilibrium, leading to new activity. A value claim had been tested and found wanting. But with the new upset of equilibrium came a new value claim, namely, the desire to understand in order to succeed. The original end-in-view had unexpected consequences which required the conceiving of a new end-in-view—not just a working model now, but a working model *and* understanding. This value claim was tested in the additional research that the boys did. It stood the test. The instrument worked.

The boys had gone through an act of valuation without, perhaps, being conscious of it. But at the conclusion of this activity there was an opportunity for the teacher to help the boys become aware of what had happened to them and what they had been through—to point out how they had learned from experience that it pays to try to understand what one is doing. A teacher who was aware of the processes by which values emerge in experience would undoubtedly be more sensitive to this opportunity than would one who believed that values can be taught through mere exposition and exhortation.

Ideal Values and the Cultural Heritage

Is it to be inferred from what has been said that values are to generate solely from the personal experience of the child? No: values generate within the experience of the human race just as they generate within individual experience. The culture within which the child lives contains a rich repository of ideal values which have been tested and refined in the experience of generations of men. This heritage should be made available to the child.

But making the child's rightful heritage available to him and imposing it upon him are two different things. To assume that the ideals evolved in racial experience are ultimate, and to ask the child to accept them passively without regard to whether they contradict the testimony of his personal experience, is to remove responsibility from him for making disciplined value judgments and to deny the validity and worth of his personal experience. As far as the child is concerned, the ideal values distilled from the experience of the race should be regarded as additional value-claims—value claims better tested and better integrated than most, and hence worthy of much more serious consideration than most—but still value claims, still to be tested and reconstructed.

The school has an obligation to help the child become acquainted with and understand the values which motivate the society of which he is a part. To fail here is to deprive the child of communication with the rest of mankind and of the vast resources of human experience. But the values prevalent in society should be presented to the child as claims only. The experience of the race is not complete until the race is dead. The child has his quota of personal experience to integrate with the experience of mankind. The values of humanity are not finally determined as long as human life still exists; the child has his share of testing and reconstructing to do.

The claims to be tested by the child, then, are both those rising in his personal experience and those proposed by others, including his own peers and those who act as the transmitters of the culture, notably his teachers. All these claims need to be further tested, to be refined and integrated, in the child's own experience. He needs the opportunity to try them out in his own living, to relate them to one another, to evaluate them in terms of the necessary steps toward their realization and in terms of the consequences they bring. From this will emerge a working set of ideals to which he is justified in committing himself.

CHAPTER VI

The Community Mode

The Problem of the Community Mode

There seems to be a common feeling in human experience that somehow the springs of man's existence flow from the community of which he is a part.

The variety of the guises in which this feeling expresses itself is enormous, ranging all the way from the totemic feasts of primitive man to the Lord's Supper; from the poet's mystic feeling, as in Walt Whitman's "Song of Myself," that his very selfhood grows from and returns to humanity, to the discovery by contemporary social psychology and cultural anthropology of the integral relation of personality and culture; from the ecclesiastical organization of the Church as a brotherhood of all men, in which they find personal evaluation, to the mystic feeling which accompanies patriotism and nationalism when they are pitched at a high—one might say shrill—key; from the classless society of communism to the sense of destiny in Hitler's "Master Race"; from the philosopher's concept of society as an organism to the well-nigh universal phenomenon of ethnocentrism with its implicit conviction that one's group determines his value.

In these various expressions one senses a greater or less degree of religious quality. It is lurking there, maimed and deformed, even in mystic nationalism, Hitlerism, and communism. The problem solved by the great world religions, and not solved either by these deformed religions or by primitive totemistic religions, is the problem of making the distinction between supreme loyalty to a limited community and supreme loyalty to an unlimited community. Of course, even the world religions in their sectarian exclusiveness are as capable of becoming deformed as was Hitlerism. But we are talking here of what they recognize at least in theory. Unless man can recognize the source of his being in the universal community rather than in a limited and special community, we are likely to conclude either that he is incapable of being religious or else that what religion he is capable of is an evil thing.

Yet, even to grow beyond the point of identification with a limited community to identification with the infinite community does not solve the religious problem. For what is to become of the individual? Is he to be swallowed up, to lose his identity in the infinite community? Neither Christianity nor democracy has been able to accept such an outlook. Christianity has struggled for almost two thousand years to establish the sacredness of individual personality; it is on this point, perhaps, that Christianity and democracy have found common ground.

But, assuming both the sacredness of the individual and the source of his being in community, the religious problem becomes one of resolving the apparent paradox of the simultaneous realization of maximum individuality and social solidarity. Communism and capitalism have surrendered to the dichotomy and have made their choices on one side or the other; for them the religious problem remains unsolved.

As we look at the religious experience of men, then, several questions come to mind.

First, can it be shown that religious experience, in one of its aspects, is essentially a recognition of community as the source of individuality?

Second, how valid is it, anyway, to look to community as the source of individuality?

Third, what is the difference between a sense of community in the arrogant, ethnocentric sense and a sense of community in the unlimited, expanding sense?

Fourth, how is the paradox of infinite individuality and an unlimited sense of community resolvable in religious experience?

These questions are so involved with one another that they can scarcely be answered serially but must be approached more or less simultaneously, with the strands separating as inquiry proceeds.

We can make a beginning, however, by taking the first question and showing that religious experience is indeed essentially a recognizing of community as the source of individual being. In order to do this, we will turn first to totemism; then to the religion of the Semites, as a stage between totemism and Christianity; and finally to Christianity itself. Having gotten this far, we can return to the other three questions.

Totemism and Semitic Religion

Totemism has been closely investigated among the primitive peoples of Australia. It exists also among the American Indians and has been connected by scholars to the great religions of antiquity, to the religions of Semitic peoples, and to European folklore. It seems to be of importance in the general history of humanity.[1]

Totemism is a system which strengthens bonds of kinship, which are defined in terms of recognized obligations, such as aid, vengeance, mourning, and exogamy. The recognition of such mutual obligations is of utmost importance to the well-being of both the individual and the group; under the precarious conditions of primitive life existence itself depends upon it.

Each clan has its totem; no two clans of the same tribe have the same totem. The totem is usually a particular species of plant or animal with which the clan identifies itself. When an individual is designated at birth as, say, a crow, he not only is a member of the

[1] See, for the Australians, Emile Durkheim, *Elementary Forms of the Religious Life*; for the Greeks, Jane Harrison, *Themis: A Study of the Social Origins of Greek Religion*; and, for the Semites, W. Robertson Smith, *The Religion of the Semites*.

crow clan, but he also learns to think of himself as somehow closely related to and even a part of the actual creature, crow.

The most sacred of all objects, for certain Australian tribes, is an oval or oblong piece of polished stone or wood known as the *churinga.* The *churinga* is carefully kept in a sacred place. The loss of it gives a clan a sense of disaster which no other event can surpass. The *churinga* plays the major part in the religious ritual of the clan.

What is the source of the *churinga*'s power and sanctity? It is nothing less than the psychological power of the sign emblazoned upon it—the representation of the totemic species. Hence the *churinga* is the symbol par excellence of kinship and social solidarity.

That sociality and religiousness are closely related if not identical in the totemic system is indicated by the relation of the sacred to the profane. Not only are the *churinga* and the totem sacred, but each individual in identifying himself with his totem partakes of its sacredness. The animal crow is sacred and so, too, is the man crow. That which is profane consists essentially of nonclan members, of youths not yet initiated, of women, and by contagion the objects associated with these individuals. Profane persons may not see, touch, or approach the *churinga.* That is, the profane is associated with that which is not admitted to full membership in the clan.

Of all rites, none display the social significance of primitive religion more than the imitative rites, which are, indeed, the root form of all other rites. The participants decorate and costume themselves in a way imitative of the totemic animal or plant. Through dancing and pageantry they express the unity of the group. They are not simply imitating kangaroos; they *are* kangaroos. They show each other that they are members of the same clan, participants in the same spirit. The participants work themselves up into a frenzy of excitement, and they end the ceremony with a feeling that their spirit has been renewed; that they have won a fresh hold on life.

On such occasions they may kill and eat the ordinarily taboo totemic animal. This is a communion in which the participants strengthen their individual souls by partaking of that which symbolizes the strength of the social group. They increase their personal strength by imbibing the spirit of the group. In one act they recognize the source of their individuality—the group—and simultaneously declare their loyalty to it.

A different development of totemic practices is to be found in the religions of the Semites—the various peoples of antiquity who inhabited the Arabian peninsula and who provide a link between the study of primitive religion and Christianity.

Sacrifice in its various forms (piacular, redemptive, covenanting, passover) is the central overt feature of Semitic religion.[2] The typical features of sacrifice are these: The sacrificial animals are slain before an altar, upon which is left a token of flesh for God. The remainder of the flesh is used for a feast in which the communicants participate with a great spirit of joviality, conviviality, and joy.

Like the totem animals of primitive society, the sacrificial animal of the Semites was ordinarily taboo and was eaten only as a part of a religious ceremony. If the idolatrous Israelites confused the golden calf with Jehovah, their confusion was understandable. If God the Father is the fountainhead of brotherhood, he can, for people not too far removed from totemism, easily be confused with the species of animal supposed to embody in itself the spirit of the group.

The economic function of the public killing of domestic animals was a consequence of the critical importance of such animals in the economy of these ancient societies. The goat, sheep, cow, and camel were basic in the economy primarily not for their flesh but for dairying, clothing, and transportation. The killing of such animals for food was not to be lightly undertaken; even when the animal was privately owned its slaughter was a matter in which the interests of the entire local community were involved. The normal meat supply was wild game; the killing of a domestic animal was

[2] See W. Robertson Smith, *The Religion of the Semites*, pp. 213-440.

simultaneously a sacrifice to God, a festive occasion, and a strictly public affair.

The assurance given by such an institution that an economically important animal would never be privately killed and eaten by its owner was vital to the welfare of the society. The sacrifice to God was one of the ways of sanctifying and ensuring the public character of the occasion. The participants were assuring one another of their intention to keep faith with one another in this essential economic matter. The token flesh upon the altar was no mere empty gesture, no mere device intended for the impressionable, but an eloquent expression of the understanding that the existence of the individual depended upon the group. The actual as opposed to the token sacrifice was the public eating of the privately owned animal; the token to God was in effect a pledge that such occasions would continue to be public. However hard it was to give up one's own valued goat or camel to feed the group, the giving of a bit of the flesh to God, who symbolized the group, served as a reminder that after all the well-being of the group made the sacrifice necessary and worth-while. And the ceremony also implied the promise that other individuals would respond in kind on other occasions.

The social function of the sacrificial meal has a basis in certain ancient customs and attitudes connected with eating and drinking. According to these, those who eat and drink together are by this very act tied to one another by a bond of mutual friendship and obligation. The Arab, for example, regarded the stranger he met on the desert as an enemy until the two ate together, after which he considered him a friend. The spirit of merriment and fellowship that prevailed at the Semitic sacrificial feasts would perhaps seem sacrilegious to modern Christians schooled in the solemnity of the Lord's Supper; yet if the meaning of this sacrament is brotherly communion, then the ancient custom expressed the spirit of the occasion.

The Christian sacrament variously known as the Eucharist, Holy Communion, and the Lord's Supper retains even for the modern communicant a great deal of the humanistic meaning of the common meal. In the communion of the celebrants is a more or less consciously expressed spirit of good fellowship, mutual respect, and love.

The Community Mode in Christianity

The foundations of the Christian idea of community are to be found both in Jesus' doctrine of love and in the founding of the early Church. Jesus in his teachings and in his own conduct taught with beautiful simplicity the principle of universal love among men. Paul in seeking to implement this principle developed the conception of the Church as the universal community within which all men are brothers.

Paul seemed to sense the essentially organic nature of society, the relation of the individual to this, and the fact that salvation consists of the creation of a good society.[3] "But now are they many members, yet but one body. And the eye cannot say unto the hand, I have no need of thee: nor again the head to the feet, I have no need of you. . . . But God hath tempered the body together . . . that the members should have the same care one for another."[4]

As an organism, society seems to have an existence of its own. It grows and declines; develops its own characteristic behavior and mentality. We speak of the mentality of the Middle Ages, of primitive man, of the twentieth century. That of which we speak is not the mere aggregate of individual minds. Individuals even in concert do not seem able to control the corporate mentality, though they may influence it. A society expresses its mentality in the culture which it generates. This is manifested in language, mores, institutions, none of which can be produced by individuals as such but only by individuals in communication.

Paul appears to have realized that a man can love his community and its qualities for their own sake, in addition to his love for

[3] See Josiah Royce, *The Problem of Christianity*, I, 61-207.
[4] *I Corinthians* 12:20-25.

specific individuals in it. A community can be worthy of such love because it can have purposes, functions, and qualities which create a good life for all its members, even though they as individuals may not be able to maintain those qualities themselves.

Paul was able to conceive of a universal community of which all men could be members and in which could be generated the qualities which would bring salvation. The doctrine of love became for him, not simply an interpersonal affair among individuals, but a love both for individuals and the organism which transcends them. All men were to treat one another as literal members of their own family. But more, they were to recognize the family itself and to love it as a person. One was to love not only all individual men but also the ideal of love itself—one was continually to expand the scope of what he recognized as his own community.

The Christian conception of the lost soul helps illuminate the idea of community.[5] Our knowledge of our selves is a function of our knowledge of and communication with our social environment. Our consciousness of the nature of our conduct and the reasons for our conduct develops through our participation in the life of the society in which we live. In comparing our own conduct with customary and established conduct sanctioned by society, we become aware of what Paul calls "the law" and of ourselves as both in harmony with and in conflict with "the law." The better we come to understand our culture, the better we know ourselves; while the better we know ourselves, the better we see the dignity, authority, and nature of the society in which we live, insofar as the latter has achieved organic quality.

What the "lost soul" loses is contact with society. He no longer can know either himself or society. Too many "lost souls" in a society disintegrate its organic quality and with it the means of the soul refinding itself. A soul becomes lost by being outside of or in conflict with society. The "uneasy conscience" is the sense of guilt that is generated by this separation—the inevitable feeling, whether justified or not, that one was somehow responsible for the

[5] Royce, *op. cit.*, I, 129-163.

schism. Since a degree of conflict even within a predominantly harmonious relationship is inevitable, sin is "original" in man.

Salvation, the return to the community, is achieved only by a new kind of socialization. To force the individual from childhood to conform can increase his chances of becoming "lost." His likely rebellion will bring him into conflict with society and thereby destroy his means of knowing himself. Love, not training, saves the individual; for, when treated with loving kindness by the members of society, he responds to, participates with, and comes to know society. Outward conformity constricts and limits; love gives vitality, substance, freshness, adaptability to community relationships. In salvation it is not "the law" but the spirit of the community that gains sovereignty over one. What dies is the lonely individual, and what is born again is the new self created by renewed belonging.

Christianity teaches that salvation cannot come by individual effort alone but is a gift of God. This expresses the fact of the inexplicable nature of the psychological processes involved in the transforming power of love. By grace of the community salvation occurs, yet the community must itself be enriched through individual contributions.

The Christian doctrine of the Trinity expresses this paradox. God is the living spirit of the community, a power which is more than the aggregate of individual contributions which create it. The Holy Ghost is the daily working of the community spirit—the concrete instances of its operations which, while particular, together pervade the whole of society. And both of these, God and the Holy Ghost, are distinguished from a third element which is yet part of their being—the Son, Jesus, the spirit of whose acts survived his physical death and became part of the organically whole spirit of the community.

The Maximum Expansion of Individuality and Community

The paradoxical but brilliant Christian concept of the relation of the individual to society is expressed by Ernst Troeltsch in the following words:

> Since . . . absolute individualism springs from the religious idea of pure-hearted self-surrender of Him who seeks men's souls and to the Fatherly Will which calls them to the vocation of being His children, so from this same fundamental idea this absolute individualism leads to just as absolute a fellowship of love among those who are united in God; from this springs an active realization of the love of God even towards strangers and enemies, because only through the revelation of absolute love can a true understanding of God be awakened and the way opened to Him. . . .
>
> Thus out of absolute individualism there arises a universalism which is equally absolute. Both these aspects of the Gospel are based entirely upon religion; their support is the thought of the Holy Divine Will of Love, and they mutually aid each other quite logically. . . . The interesting point for us is simply the fact that absolute individualism and universalism spring directly out of the religious idea, and that this fact has, sociologically, a double aspect. Both require each other. For individualism only becomes absolute through the ethical surrender of the individual to God . . . and on the other hand, in possession of the Absolute, individual differences merge into an unlimited love whose prototype is the Father-God Himself, to whom souls are drawn and in whom they are united.[6]

Here the relation of individual and community is expressed in the traditional language of Christianity. The paradox of the maximum but simultaneous realization of both individuality and community is resolved through God as the source of both. Yet it is to be noted that God is here held to be the prototype of universal love, and that individuality and community become realized simultaneously, not only through the mutual love of God and his children but also through the love of the children for one another.

In the Christian view there are two senses—actual and ideal—in which love accounts for the simultaneous realization of individuality and community. The actual loving relations that exist among men promote the individuality of each and the community of all. But love is capable of being extended in a degree and in ways not now realized nor even conceived. We cannot even be sure that what we now recognize as love will be so recognized in the light of further experience. Hence we must infinitely keep moving in

[6] Ernst Troeltsch, *The Social Teachings of the Christian Church,* pp. 56-57. Copyright 1931 by The Macmillan Company. Reprinted by permission.

the direction of an improved and reconstructed practice and concept of love. This is love in the ideal sense, and it is expressed metaphorically in the concept of God as the prototype of love.

In Christianity men must not only love one another, but they must love the ideal of love itself. The brotherhood of man depends upon the fatherhood of God. From a naturalistic standpoint this means that the ideal of love fathers the practice of love.

Community is a present actuality insofar as love is existent in the world. There are existing communities to which individuals belong and by virtue of which they are able to recognize themselves as distinct selves. Membership in family groups, neighborhood groups, occupational groups, various interest groups, and political units is experienced in greater or less degree by most individuals. In proportion as there is belonging, there are concrete communities pervaded by love, common purpose, and creativity. This is expressed in the concept of the Holy Ghost.

But at the same time there is, when religion prevails in life, a demand that the limited community or communities to which a man belongs be expanded. To become absolutely loyal to any one community as it exists is also to become devoted to exclusiveness. Members of other communities are excluded, classed as profane, and love is limited. Hence the ideal of a continually expanding community is essential to the religious spirit. Even a community whose membership includes all men now living could not be taken as final, for to do so would rule out the possibility of growth toward modes of social life that man has not yet experienced.

Hence community is an ideal concept as well as an actuality. If its present actuality is expressed in the idea of the Holy Ghost, its ideal nature is expressed by the idea of the Father.[7]

The simultaneous maximum development of both community

[7] If God is the ideal and actual community when religion is in the community mode, he is the creative social act when religion is in the valuational mode, and other meanings are expressed in other modes. Such meanings may interpenetrate and support one another; e. g., it can be shown that creativity depends upon community and community upon creativity. In the various religious modes are encountered various aspects of the one God.

and individuality, in our age so often seen as inherently opposed to one another, is conceptually possible in Christianity because the context in which they appear is seen as one of love rather than conflict. When there is love the individual participates with and comes to know his community, and the community to know him. When there is conflict the community is shattered; men are lost to one another and cannot know either one another or their community. In coming to know the community, the individual comes to know himself; he develops a picture of himself as seen through the eyes of the community, and he is in a position thereby to direct his growth and increase the worth of his individuality. The lost individual loses knowledge of self and behaves in ways that destroy selfhood.

In coming to know the individual, the community learns to understand and appreciate him. He becomes valued both for his own sake and for what he can contribute. His defects as well as his strength become apparent to the community; but because it knows and understands him, it wishes to help him grow where he is weak and contribute where he is strong. Under such conditions the community does not seek conformity, but rather cherishes what is valuable and unique.

The simultaneous flourishing of both individuality and belongingness is conceptually and actually possible in a social context of love. To realize this conceptually and actually is the basic problem of our age.

The Creative Social Act as the Source of Selfhood and Community

We return once more to the creative social act as the basic fact of religious experience. In the creative social act are embodied the qualities by which both selfhood and community can be simultaneously realized.

There is evidence from the sober findings of contemporary social psychology that the creative social act is quite literally the source of one's being. Not only is the social act the creator of the individual's personality; it also creates that which most distinguishes him as a man—his very mind.

A man is born into this world equipped with a body and a central nervous system of superior potentialities. But at birth he does not yet have a mind. Neither does he have a self nor a personality. All of these are yet to be developed. Will they develop simply by further growth of the physical equipment that is already there? If we could perform the experiment of placing this child in a complete social vacuum, would we upon returning to him years later find that he had developed within himself his own mind, selfhood, and personality?

The closest approximations to such an impossible experiment are the several authenticated cases of children who survived several years of living in the wilds after being abandoned in infancy. These children were found to be unable to talk, to recall previous experiences, to solve simple mental problems. Furthermore, despite all efforts to educate and train them, they *never* developed any considerable mental competence. They not only had failed to develop minds during their years of isolation, but they had even lost the potentiality of doing so.[8]

The reasons for such an outcome can be understood in the light of present psychological knowledge. Without linguistic and conceptual tools, one cannot think. Without making the human culture a part of one's being, one cannot be human. At birth not only the mind but also the self or personality still are to be developed through human association. Every person has a role to play in the life of the community of which he is a part. Growing up is essentially a process of discovering and creating that role. That role, whatever it is, defines one's selfhood and personality. At birth the child's role has not yet been defined. He does not yet have a name; he has not yet established his particular kind of relations with his immediate family. While his moral convictions, manners, aesthetic

[8] Arnold Gesell, *Wolf Child and Human Child.* (New York: Harper & Brothers, 1941).

tastes, social status, might be predicted, they have not yet, as far as he is concerned, been established.

The fact that there is some predictability as to these things only serves to call attention to human association as the source of selfhood. We can predict not because we know the child as a self but because we know his community; know its mores, its culture, its demands. For example, an American boy raised in China by a Chinese family will be, in selfhood and personality, a Chinese. Yet of course the individual is not a mere reflection of his culture. He has a role to play *in* the culture, a more or less unique role which defines his personality. Interaction with the social environment is what uncovers and creates that role in all its uniqueness.

Inadequate as our understanding of personality and mind still is today, we do have some notion of the psychological processes by which selfhood and mind are created through human association.[9]

The key seems to be the occurrence of role-playing in the social acts of men. One is able to respond appropriately to another, regardless of whether the social relation is a competitive or a cooperative one, because one is able to assume the role of the other and internally to complete the other's acts while they are still in their incipient stages.

How do two men rolling a log together, for example, coordinate their actions? Each must not only actually do his part, that is perform his overt role in the joint act, but also he must internally play out the role of the other. He must, using the initial stages of the other's actions as a guide, be able to know what the other is going to do next; know how the other is going to complete his act. The first individual internally but not overtly completes the act of the other. By doing this he can adjust his own overt act to coordinate with the act of the other. He finds his own overt role by internally enacting the role of the other.

Mind or, better, minded behavior arises in social acts in the fol-

[9] For the pioneer study of how mind, selfhood, and community emerge within the social act, see George H. Mead, *Mind, Self and Society*, upon whose analysis I base the following pages.

lowing way: At the pre-minded biological level where role-taking is absent, behavior consists merely of the physical resolution of the tensions created in the immediate contact of organism and environment. In role-playing the organism anticipates the responses both of the natural and social environment, and adjusts its behavior accordingly. The ability thus to take the role of the other is facilitated by the development in social acts of language, which makes possible symbolic modes of completing the other's acts. As a flexible yet systematic linguistic structure emerges, the power and virtuosity of the individual in his playing of roles increases. In taking the role of the other (including that of the physical environment), the individual tests the consequences of possible courses of action in imagination and is thus able to plan and control behavior in a way that we recognize as minded.

The self emerges simultaneously in this process. In experimenting with many roles, the individual discovers and creates the role which defines him as a self. He selects from, responds to, and integrates many roles in finding his own role. Furthermore, he becomes an object to himself. By taking the roles of other persons, he is able to look back upon his own role. He sees his acts through the eyes of others and becomes a self to himself for the first time. By finding a vantage point from which to view himself, he is able to evaluate himself, or better the pattern of his life role, and modify or reconstruct it accordingly. He wants to be able to see himself as others do. To be able to do so is the touchstone of contact with reality, as the findings of contemporary depth psychology suggest.

The foregoing throws a new light upon the significance of the creative social act. It helps show the real sense in which the creative social act is the source, the creator, of both selfhood and community. In their relations with one another men learn to take the roles of one another. In taking the roles of one another they come to understand one another. To understand is not to condone, but it is to sympathize and to wish to help. In short, it is to love. Role-playing admits the other into one's recognized community. As men interact with one another in creative social activity, the scope of their role-playing and hence the scope of their personally recognized community expands indefinitely.

But in this same process the individual experiments with possible roles which may define his selfhood. He tries them out, integrates them, stands aside and evaluates his own role from the standpoint of others, seeks to determine both the role in society others expect of him and the role he wants for himself, and tries to integrate the two. Thus he continuously keeps finding a new self by surrendering his old self to the creative social act.

The infinite and continuous expansion of both community and selfhood is a realizable ideal through devotion to the creative social act. By associating with many kinds of personalities in many kinds of cooperative acts, the individual experiences a variety of roles which may be integrated into his own personality. It is to the interest of men that they protect and cultivate the uniqueness of one another, so that each may find a richer and more varied society in which to build his own personality.

CHAPTER VII

The Community Mode: Education

The Educational Goal

PARTICIPATION in the creative social act is the key to the child's experience of religion in its community mode. Through such participation a double goal can be realized. In the first place, the child can experience a sense of belonging to an ever-expanding community. And in the second place, he can, by finding his role in the community, experience the continual expansion of his personality. The social act creates an expanding community for the child, and he finds a self within that community and expands with it.

The school's task is to promote both community and individuality in the greatest possible degree. In terms of community, the task is both to strengthen the child's sense of belonging and to increase the scope of the community that the child is disposed to recognize as his own. In terms of personality, the task is to help the child develop depth, strength, integrity, and versatility of selfhood.

The child needs both a community to be loyal to and a self to be true to. There is a matter of fundamental integrity in the double sense of both honesty and wholeness. The child has a need to belong somewhere. Without a group of his own he is lost and disoriented. He literally "goes to pieces" because, lacking a stable role to play in a definite community, he leaps from role to role, secure and at home in none of them, seeking but never finding the one to which he belongs. His behavior is accordingly inconsistent and erratic. He is "riding off in all directions at once" because he can commit himself to no one direction. He displays the symptoms of a thoroughly disintegrated personality. By finding a community to which he can be true, he also acquires a role to which he can be true. To be true to one's self means that one has stabilized his role in society. While he may and should be flexible, he does not contradict his own character from one act to the next. He is capable of being honest with himself and with society because he has found a role of such dignity and a self of such effectiveness that he feels he can be true to them.

Yet, even though the goal is to help the child find both a community and a self to which he can be loyal, still there is no one community nor any ultimate self to which the child should become irrevocably committed for all time. The ultimate goal is to keep both his community and his self continually growing. The distinction is between community and ethnocentrism on the one hand, and between being true to one's self and self-centered arrogance on the other. Community and self-giving are complementary aspects of an expanding situation; ethnocentrism and self-centeredness of a static or contracting situation. Consequently neither community nor selfhood, important as they are, should be the ultimate value to which the child becomes committed. Loyal to some finite community he must be, and loyal to himself. But these must be loyalties qualified by humility and by readiness for change, because the ultimate loyalty must be reserved solely for that which continually expands community and selfhood—the creative social act.

The situation in respect to the community mode is analogous to the one encountered in respect to the valuational mode. In the latter mode, we are confronted by the paradoxical situation in which the child must be helped to develop ideal values to which he dedicates his life conduct, but which he is nevertheless ready to give up whenever participation in the creative social act indicates a needed reconstruction of value. Just as the child, in the valuational mode, becomes committed yet not committed to finite sets of ideal values, so, in the community mode, he becomes committed yet not committed to a finite community and self. In both cases the ultimate object of loyalty is the creative social act.

The nature of original or ultimate sin can be expressed in different modes. In the valuational mode sin is the claim to ultimate knowledge of what is right and good; in the community mode sin is the substitution of either group- or self-centeredness for the spirit of community. In either case, what is sinned against is the creative social act.

The Effect of Cooperation and Competition upon the Expansion of the Child's Community

Living and working with others in voluntary cooperative activities is the basic kind of experience which can promote the child's sense of community.

Such experience helps the child learn to appreciate and respect the personalities of others. The primary requisite for the growth of such appreciation and respect is the existence of a common goal. The problems involved in a group's finding common goals for itself will be taken up on a later page—for the moment we wish to note the effect that the existence of a common goal has upon the personalities and attitudes of the participants.

Consider the contrast between the behavior of individuals who have found a common goal and the behavior of those who find themselves in an essentially competitive relation to one another. For example, what are the contrasting attitudes toward differences in the other person? In the competitive situation the individual is likely either to be envious and covetous of the other's uniqueness or else to regard him with contempt and a feeling of superiority. Which of these attitudes it shall be is determined by whether the other's difference gives him an advantage or disadvantage in the competitive struggle.

Competing individuals have every reason to regard one another with a certain degree of hositility. The fact that they are trying to get the same thing puts them in opposition to one another. Each regards the other's success as his failure. If the other has some desirable quality or ability, he has an advantage in the race. One is envious of his special gift and would like it for himself. Furthermore, one is likely to scheme and plot in the effort to find some way to neutralize the other's talent. To create a situation where his talent is no longer relevant or useful, even to rob him of it in some way, become prime matters of strategy.

On the other hand, if the other has some deficiency or weakness, he is at a disadvantage in the competitive race. One's strategy then is to find every possible way to play upon, to take advantage of, the other's particular weakness. Now situations are manipulated in such a way as to make the other's peculiarity stand out in disproportionate prominence. We strike him where we know he is weak and try to by-pass the points at which we know he is strong. And because success is felt to be proof of superiority, we regard his weakness with contempt.

The situation is different if the participants feel that their goal is held in common. Now the success of one is felt to be the success of all. What attitudes toward differences in the other person does this generate? If the other has a special gift, we are glad and thankful. Here is a contribution to the joint effort—a hope and a resource for all of us. We seek to influence situations in such a way that the other can capitalize upon his talent to the fullest extent. We find ways to help him sharpen up and strengthen his special ability. On the other hand, if he has some weakness, there is nothing to encourage us, as there is in the competitive situation, to take advantage of it. We want to help him with his difficulty. We want to strengthen him so that he can play his part in the common enterprise. When the welfare of each person is bound to that of the other in some common enterprise, there is little to make us compete for talents and resources. If we have something the other needs or lacks, we readily share it with him so that he can be more effective in his work.

When goals are held in common, the desirably unique qualities of the other person are cherished and cultivated. Difference, not conformity, becomes a positive value, to be encouraged as a potential contribution. In contrast, to dare to be different in a competitive society or group is often regarded with a jaundiced eye. Conformity is a virtue because any deviation is a potential threat when persons feel essentially in competition with one another.

In short, the existence of common goals breeds attitudes of love and respect for the personality of the other. We cherish what is good in him; we take a sympathetic attitude and desire to help in respect to his lacks and needs; we encourage him to be different; we help him cultivate his possibilities and realize his potentialities.

The foregoing remarks would not be pertinent were it not for the fact that in the past the schools have placed a premium upon competition as the primary method of motivating learning. This has become such a characteristic feature of the school and is so taken for granted that we are scarcely aware of how completely the beast has devastated our educational system.

For example, it is seldom realized that the controversies which rage over the question of homogeneous grouping according to the I.Q. could not exist were there not an implicit assumption that competition is the normal procedure of the school. Only on such an assumption could it be regarded as an advantage to have all children in a given group cut to a single intellectual pattern. The unexpressed, unconscious consideration here is that the differences between children must be minimized so that the competitive battle to learn can be something other than a farce. It spoils the fun when children are so grotesquely different in ability that no really competitive race can be run. "How can I motivate them *all*?" cries the teacher in despair, finding that the goal to be competed for is too easy for some and too hard for others. What the educator sees, quite rightly, is that under competitive conditions no teacher can do justice to widely varying abilities. In the competitive classroom all children are expected to reach the same goal through the same processes. But they cannot.

Such a consideration would not bother anyone who saw the classroom situation as one in which children work together toward common goals. Each, regardless of ability, can find a unique role to play in the common enterprise—a role that can challenge his abilities, whatever they may be. Homogeneous grouping, on the basis of the I. Q. or any other basis except common interest, is seen as a disadvantage because there is less variety of personality with which to fill the many roles that need to be filled.

Homogeneous grouping is a nefarious practice—a sin against the creative social act and the ideal of an expanding community. It creates in the children either feelings of exclusiveness or of envy; it deprives them of experiences in reaching out to and working with all kinds of other children; it limits the variety of contribution to the creative social act.

Homogeneous grouping and its evils are mentioned here because they are symptomatic of the school's orientation toward competitive methods which shatter rather than promote community. Other symptoms exist—the system of rewards and punishments as the motivation for competition; the typical seating plans, with the children so obviously arranged for individualistic rather than cooperative work; and, perhaps most telling of all, the tendency to put a premium upon conformity rather than deviation. Conformity is the external form of community without its spirit. Conformity answers to without satisfying the hunger for community, or is imposed when the dangers of division and revolt are felt to be great. In view of these unhealthy symptoms, the question arises whether the schools can reverse their orientation and build a curriculum based upon recognition by the children of common interests and common goals.

The Achievement of a Community of Value

Acceptance of a common goal as motivation for some specific activity is dependent upon the members of a group being able to establish a community of value. When children are in the policy-forming stages of an activity, there is likely to be a clash of individual wills, interests, and personalities. The children do not all have the same problems, nor do they all attach the same weight to whatever possible problems are being considered as bases for further work.

What is behind such clashes? While the specific causes may be legion, in the broadest interpretation a clash of wills is a manifestation of incompatible values held by the contending parties. For example, Helen is opposed to the proposals being made by some of the boys in the class that the group study how machines work because as a girl her past experiences have built in her a set of values which affect her attitudes toward and interest in machinery and how it works. Each child has a unique background of personal experience which determines his value structure. This influences his attitudes, sensitivities, interests, needs, and desires. When children disagree upon policy as they plan their activities, this is a signal that contending values are at stake. An effort to establish a community of value is indicated.

The school can promote no skill more important than the ability to achieve, given conflict at the start, a community of value. We live in a society and in an age in which conflict is an overwhelming fact. Society is divided along innumerable lines into groups which have different interests at stake. The conflicting interests and experiences of these groups create for each its own structure of value. Looking at the world from the perspective of its value structure, each group is unable to see a universe of value uniting all. The differences among groups tend to be settled by coercion. The great need of our time is to develop attitudes, habits, and skills which enable men to communicate their partial value claims to one another, to consider them together, and to move toward a community of value.

Consequently, when children clash, when a struggle of wills appears in the midst of the choosing, planning, and organizing of their activities, not a catastrophe but an educational opportunity has arisen.

And how well are such opportunities capitalized upon in many schools? Often the teacher, disturbed by the possibility of disorder and chaos, establishes an authoritarian regime and settles the conflict arbitrarily. Sometimes the group and the teacher permit the most aggressive faction to take charge and organize the group. Or the situation can simply end in disorderly chaos.

All of these solutions are destructive of religious quality. In each case one arbitrary force or another takes charge and substitutes itself for the creativity of the group. Anarchy is as arbitrary in its effect as authoritarianism—the willfulness of individual impulses is as bad as the willfulness of a dictator.

The group, with the help of its teacher, needs to find a way of settling its differences which will release, not destroy, creativity. What about compromise, then?

The recognition of creativity as a primary value helps show that even compromise is not a satisfactory method of resolving conflict. In compromise there is no fundamental change in the respective interests at stake. The parties to the conflict still hold to their interests, but find it politic to agree to arrangements which will only partly realize their interests and which in some degree distort them. They can support such compromise policies only with something less than full enthusiasm. No matter how sincere the intention to live up to a compromise agreement may be, the individual cannot put his heart into it because lurking within him is still his loyalty to his original uncompromised interest.

This is not to say that children should never use compromise when, in making choices, their interests clash. It is far better to compromise than either to let the more aggressive personalities prevail or to let anarchy develop. Both anarchy and aggressive domination are more destructive of creativity than is compromise. Compromise saves for the individual at least some of what he has at stake, while the arbitrary impositions of others in both authoritarian and anarchical situations may destroy the possibility of realizing any of his interests.

But a fuller release of creativity can result if the method of compromise is replaced by the method of interpersuasion leading toward consensus.[1] In this method a clash of interests is regarded by

[1] There perhaps is some significance in the fact that a *religious* group, the Quakers, has seen this so clearly and has tried to practice it so assiduously.

the participants as an occasion not for compromising but for transforming interests. If the interests of the participants can be transformed in such a way that all concerned feel the new interests to be their own, then they can agree to a common policy and carry it out wholeheartedly without the conscious or unconscious reservations that must result from compromise. Transformation of interests can occur if the participants can learn to examine one another's interests, to consider the experiences of the other leading him to those interests, to look for the values the other one seems to see, and to integrate these various values. This requires a process of communication in which each makes clear his experiences and his feelings about them to the other, and in which each tries to understand what the other is expressing.

When values clash, each contending group or individual must do at least three things. First, he must present to the others a statement and analysis of the experiences he has had which lead him to the values he holds. Second, he must be willing to listen and understand while the other parties to the conflict present their own statements. And third, assuming that as a result of the first two steps the persons involved now share a common core of experience, they must use this experience as the basis for seeking a community of value.

The success of such an effort at communication depends upon role-playing. There is a joint effort directed at making it possible for each of the contending groups to put itself in the place of the others and vicariously experience the events which led the others to their partial values. When an individual spreads his previous experience before others for their examination and evaluation, he is adopting an attitude which others recognize as objective. He is, in effect, inviting others to see why he believes as he does and to help fill in the gaps in his experience so that he can see whether a change of belief is indicated.

Such objectivity on the part of the participant requires, however, that the material he lays before the others be treated with care and respect. The others must be equally objective in reporting the kinds of experiences they feel are needed to supplement those presented by the first individual. The others, too, need the gaps in their experience filled in, and they must learn to recognize this. It is no exaggeration to say that the task of coming to valuational consensus is essentially one of communication in which the participants seek through role-playing to fill in the gaps in one another's experience.

The following illustrates the point:

The members of the second grade had raised vegetables in a small plot outside their room and sold them to the school cafeteria for $1.75. They were proud of their accomplishment and feeling possessive about their money. Now the question arose of what to do with this enormous wealth.

"Salt 'em up!" said Pedro.

"Naw, money is waste time," protested Henry. "Better to spend."

There was an immediate division of the class between those who would save and those who would spend. The arguments came forth.

"Once I got ten cents. My ma told me to save. I bought candy. Next day I was sorry. My friends went to a movie but I couldn't. No money."

"We should wait until third grade, and save more. Then we can do something big."

"But before, many guys got moved to other classes. Better spend now!"

At this point the teacher wondered whether a solution might be to spend part and save part of the money. The discussion turned to consideration of specific ways of doing this.

One proposal which won wide and enthusiastic backing was to spend some money at once for a class party. But there was objection. Some children pointed out this had been done last year and now they had nothing to show for it.

One child recalled that some of the other classes, which had raised flowers instead of vegetables, had often given flowers to the second-graders, who had nothing to put them in but old glass jars. "We can buy paint and paint 'em up!" he proposed.

Some children pointed out that this would preserve the value of having something lasting which one child had called attention to. Some pointed out also that the second-graders could give some of the painted jars to the classes which had so generously given them flowers.

The class felt strongly moved in this direction, but there was still objection from one group which wanted to save and from another group which wanted the fun of a party.

Finally, one child pointed out that if only part of the money were now spent for paint and the rest saved, the class could, on the very last day of school, have a party. This suggestion seemed to resolve the various claims, and was accepted as the solution.

In this example, competing value claims brought the children into conflict. But communication brought a rounding out of each child's experience. A community of experience brought a community of value. The value of saving became integrated with the social values involved in having a party. The value of doing something to improve the appearance of the classroom became integrated with the value of contributing generously to others. One notes in the discussion the extent of recall of both individual and group experience.

In the end the group conserved values which overarched the more partial claims originally advanced, and this was done largely through each individual's helping others share with him the experiences that caused him to hold the values he did. The teacher was able to promote an atmosphere in which such an objective give and take of ideas could take place. Objective discussion was more "fashionable" in the eyes of the children than mere verbal aggression and conquest.

Submission and Discovery of the Self in the Creative Social Act

Of all the persons in a given classroom, perhaps the one who typically has most difficulty in subordinating his ego to the creative social act is the teacher himself. Tradition is such that the burden of authority placed upon him by the community weighs all too heavily upon his shoulders. Not sure of himself, not sure that he has the strength or ability to carry such authority, he often overacts in his effort to bear it.

Yet if a teacher is to cultivate religious quality in the classroom community of which he should be a part, he must display religious quality in his own conduct. He must be able and willing to submit himself to the creative social act and to let it produce what it will. A guide to his class, a contributor to the social act, he must be, but a killer of the act, never. To play God, to be the final authority, to impose his will, is to slay the creative social act itself and with it the source of whatever good can be produced in his classroom. The possibility that he may one day be asked by his children a simple factual question that he cannot answer is a great bugaboo to many a teacher. He does not realize he could show both wisdom and teaching skill by a simple answer of "I don't know—let's see if we can find out."

The following illustrates a situation in which a teacher, by failing to submit to the creative social act, became confused and lost. The class was a fifth-grade group.

Mrs. Rogers came to class prepared to present some demonstrations which would show the students some principles about the shape, rotation, and revolution of the earth. She was equipped with globes, oranges, candles, string, and other materials.

She asked a child to stand before the class, representing the sun. A second child was asked to move in a circle around the first, thus demonstrating the revolution of the earth around the sun. The second child was asked to spin on her own axis while she circled the sun, thus demonstrating the earth's rotation as well as its revolution.

To clinch this idea, Mrs. Rogers asked the earth-child first to spin only, then to revolve only, then to do both together. This cycle was gone through several times until the children were sure of the difference between revolution and rotation, and of the simultaneous operation of both.

The children were interested and began to ask questions. These gradually increased in number and in difficulty until they amounted to a veritable flood of pertinent and not easily answered questions. By the time Mrs. Rogers reached the mid-point in her lesson she was all but overwhelmed by the questions and was showing signs of becoming confused. The following are samples of the kinds of questions asked:

1. If the earth spins so fast why don't we feel it?

2. Why does the sun move right along with me when I walk down the street?

3. If the sun is so hot, why do we get colder when we go high in the air? Doesn't that take us closer to the sun and shouldn't we get warmer?

Mrs. Rogers tried to answer each question, one by one, at the time it arose. But each answer only raised a host of new questions. Not only were the questions difficult to answer, but many of them seemed to exceed the limits of the teacher's knowledge. As she became increasingly confused, she oscillated between attempting to give full, complete, and definitive answers to each question, on the one hand, and ruling out the questions as irrelevant or too time-consuming, on the other. She finally ended the lesson with the comment that tomorrow she would answer some of the questions for which there had been no time today, and that after that the children would study about some of the other planets.

Had the teacher not misconceived her role, she could have used the children's questions and their interest as the starting point for creative and constructive activity. She could have said, not "I'll tell you tomorrow," but "Let's organize these questions and see what we can find out about them."

She would have no way of knowing in advance what would come of such a move. Not only might some of the answers have been unknown to her, but, even more significantly, she could not know in advance just what plans she and the children might end up with, what projects they might undertake, how successfully the various projects would be completed. We would want her to have enough competence and general background in her subject to be an adequate help and guide. But for her to know the outcome in advance would be another matter. Only by joining with her children to push into unknown territory could she do justice to the situation. As it was, she killed creativity at its birth.

Sadly enough, in destroying the source of good she became a lost soul herself. She ended the period feeling confused and inadequate, whereas if she had joined with the children, had taken them into her confidence and planned with them, there is every likelihood that she would have ended the period feeling both thrilled and adequate. In letting his ego stand in the way of the creative social act, one destroys the source of his own selfhood.

The following is an example of a teacher who, like Mrs. Rogers, destroyed creativity. But unlike Mrs. Rogers she remained master of the situation at all times. The children were fourth-graders.

Mrs. Murphy introduced the idea of the usefulness of maps by referring to a trip made the previous day by the children. She asked the children to suggest what maps are for and what they tell.

Mrs. Murphy probed a little to get the children to extend and refine their answers. She approved some and rejected others. She summarized their responses in excellently organized lists on the blackboard. These lists conformed exactly with ones Mrs. Murphy had already placed in her lesson plan.

Mrs. Murphy asked the children to illustrate the points just made by drawing maps of a place most familiar to them—their own classroom. The class discussed the items to be included in the map. The final decision as to the appropriateness of each item was made by the teacher rather than the children. The children then each drew identical maps by following the teacher as she produced the map item by item at the blackboard.

Each item was discussed with the children before it was added. Then Mrs. Murphy asked volunteers to come forward to indicate in red or blue chalk the seats occupied respectively by boys and girls. Those at their seats used crayons for the same purpose. Mrs. Murphy designated the colors to be used. This done, she produced a large outline map of the neighborhood she had prepared ahead of time. This was posted before the group, and volunteers came forward to locate on the map familiar neighborhood spots. The lesson ended with an assignment for homework. Each child was to make and bring to school a map locating his house in its neighborhood.

Throughout the lesson the activities of Mrs. Murphy were perfectly organized and she was very sure of what she was doing. Her work showed meticulous preparation, and she carried out everything according to plan. Her manner with the children was poised, gentle, and objective. The children accepted her leadership with alacrity and interest, yet as each child made his contribution, he kept his eyes fixed upon Mrs. Murphy to see how it would be accepted. She was able smoothly to channel their responses into her prearranged plan.

The above creates the illusion of a soundly and efficiently taught lesson. The teacher is well prepared and well organized. She is clear as to her objectives. She uses good psychological principles, such as moving from the more to the less familiar. Her relation with the children is objective and businesslike. Yet the children are carrying little responsibility for thinking and evaluating. Although they are doing the same things at the same times, each works individually at his own seat. The work is mechanical rather than creative, individualistic rather than cooperative. There is little challenge to the children because their work is so closely directed that they can scarcely make mistakes. The atmosphere is so sanitary that the children are protected from experiencing either much failure or much success.

This could just as well have been a pupil-planned and cooperatively executed enterprise. The teacher could have planned with the children instead of pulling from them plans she already had in mind. The children could have helped one another with their maps. They could have set up a committee to evaluate maps and send them back to their makers for revision. Instead of stressing uniformity of production, individuals could have experimented with a variety of approaches to the problem. They could have stimulated one another with the variety of their attempts. By having greater responsibilities, the children could have experienced greater successes. If the danger of making mistakes had been more real, there could have been more challenge. Through this all the teacher could have moved as a guide and helper instead of a master mind.

By personally assuming responsibilities which should have been left to the creative social act, this teacher effectively prevented anything unexpected happening. This was a protection against failure. But it was also a barrier to the release of creative energy. In the name of efficiency the teacher dared to predetermine outcomes and destroy creativity. Though not intending arrogance, she persuaded herself that she could personally guarantee better outcomes than could be achieved through group planning and effort.

Her personal tragedy was that by dominating the situation she prevented her own self-realization. Despite all her preparation and effort, she could get from her children only mechanical responses to her demands. She could not experience the satisfaction and thrill of having stimulated children to unexpected varieties of individual and group accomplishment.

In contrast, the following shows what happens when both teachers and children submit themselves to the creative social act. Again, the children were fourth-graders.

The children had just finished listening to a radio dramatization of a fairy story. The story involved a little girl who, getting into difficulties with her parents, runs away from home. In the woods she comes to a house, which she enters, only to find it empty. Queer things begin happening in this house, climaxed by the appearance of a poor old beggar with a white beard, for whom the girl performs a kind act. The old man immediately turns into a brownie, who then helps reunite the little girl and her parents.

Miss Roberts asked the children whether they liked the story. Since there was an affirmative response, the teacher suggested that perhaps some children would like to tell what parts they liked best. One liked the queer things that happened in the house, another the reuniting of the family, and so on. Miss Roberts asked the children if they would like to act out their own version of the story. The children responded enthusiastically.

Since there would be no script and no set lines or action, it would be difficult to keep the continuity of the story as it was acted out. Hence the teacher suggested that first the children plan the main episodes to be dramatized. One child suggested that the first episode should be "Lenka Goes Away." This idea was immediately accepted by the group.

A boy suggested that the next episode should be called "The Crazy House." The class groaned its protest. But the youngster was given a chance to explain his choice. He said that the things which happened in the house were not things that could really happen and just seemed crazy to him.

A girl said that the scene should be called "The Magic Hut." This seemed to catch the spirit of enchantment in the scene that the group wished to capture, for there was a chorus of approval. But the boy still objected that it was "Crazy." The teacher said, "I think we must all agree with George that these things could not really happen. But perhaps we all like to pretend sometimes that such things do happen." This remark seemed to preserve both the value of reality that George wanted and the value of fantasy that the group wanted. At any rate, "The Magic Hut" title was accepted by the group and even George seemed satisfied.

Proceeding in a similar way, evaluating the suggestions that came up, the group worked out their complete list of episodes.

This done, Miss Roberts asked what else would have to be done befor the dramatization could actually begin. Someone pointed out that a cast of players would have to be chosen. The children began naming the characters involved and these were placed on the board. The children immediately began calling out names of children they wanted for each part. It sounded like more or less of a popularity contest. The teacher quieted the group and remarked that, rather than choosing one's friend for a favorite part, it might be better to make sure that the right person was chosen for the right part.

The first character to be cast was the mother, and the teacher asked what sort of person would be needed to play such a part. One child thought she should be a tall person. Another thought she should be someone who acted "grown-up." The class nominated several children and finally selected a large, mature-looking girl for the part. Next the part of the brownie was considered. One child thought he should be a boy, and small. Another thought he should be a dark-complexioned, and another that he should be a quick rather than a slow-moving boy. A small, lively looking youngster was finally picked for the part. The casting of the other parts was done in a similar way.

Miss Roberts again asked what else would have to be done before dramatization could begin. Someone said, "We need to get together the different things the actors need." The teacher explained that the correct word for these things was "properties" and that the term "props" could be used for short. The children immediately began using the new terms in their discussion. Props that would be needed were named and listed on the board. Few or none of the necessary items were available in the room, but the children began suggesting substitutes. Someone said fountain pens and automatic pencils could do for the pile of jewels in the play. A dozen or so such items were offered at once by as many children. One child's briefcase was proffered as a substitute for a bag that was to hold coal and ashes. Blackboard erasers and bits of paper became the coal and ashes. The old beggar's white beard was no sooner mentioned than one boy whipped out a white handkerchief, arranged it under his chin, twisted the corners, and looped them over his ears.

The children could now think of no further preparations that needed to be made. The cast quickly assembled and organized itself for the first scene.

Before they began, the teacher asked one child to recall, out loud, the main action of the scene. Other children supplemented his account at the points where he made important omissions. The characters then simply launched into the dramatization, making up their lines and action as they went along. They were eager and enthusiastic. Each actor responded, on the whole, appropriately to what the actor just before him had done or said, yet at the same time pushed the story along. There were a few awkward pauses, but on such occasions suggestions from others were quickly forthcoming. Those not acting were intent in following every move.

Every child seemed caught up in the spirit that the group itself was generating. One boy, Philip—who was playing the father—illustrates what was happening to all. He was a boy who all during the semester had exhibited a serious degree of stammering. Now, as the father, he took his cues with scarcely any hesitation and produced his lines, making them up, of course, as did the others. But there was no actual stammering. Only once or twice did his chin quiver as though he were about to stammer.

As the scene moved along, the audience was not able to remain in its seats. Almost every child stood on tiptoe to see better. When the scene ended, there was considerable noise and confusion, caused by the desire of so many to make suggestions for modifying and improving the scene. The cast seemed glad to get these suggestions.

Only one scene was done on this occasion. It was decided to continue with the other scenes on the next day, and gradually to get the action "set" on the basis of such trials as that completed today.

Here was a teacher who contributed to the creative social act, but who nevertheless did not try to find in her own person a substitute for the act itself. Her contributions to the group enterprise were significant and helpful. But she helped in a way that stimulated thought and activity, not in a way that brought thought and activity to a conclusion. She pointed to possibilities instead of answers. When she asked questions her intention was to promote exploration, not guessing games as to the content of her own mind.

When she helped the children organize the ideas they contributed, the effect was to place the children in a better position for actually carrying them out. When she supplied them with vocabulary, she was not so much interested in building vocabulary for its own sake as in giving them a tool the better with which to do their own thinking.

She made the nice distinction between leadership which stimulates or releases the leadership potentialities of others and leadership which in assuming responsibility removes it from others. While maintaining leadership, she still kept herself subordinate to the creative social act. Her aim was to promote creativity, not to dominate the situation.

The participants, including the teacher, who thus willingly surrendered their egos to the creative social act must have found therein self-fulfilment. This is most strikingly illustrated in the case of Philip, the boy who stammered. He allowed himself to be carried away by the group's creativity. And he found there a new self which no longer stammered. Undoubtedly, after the spirit of the occasion was gone, Philip's old self would return to haunt him. But he had taken a step toward a permanent change. As for the teacher, she too was finding a satisfying role, a recognition of her adequacy in encouraging such productive enterprise in others.

The example also shows how reconstruction of values occurs through participation in the creative social act. One could guess that changes were taking place in the children's attitudes toward dramatization, toward school, toward one another. The most explicit instance occurred when George, during the choosing of the title for the second scene, set forth his value of common-sense realism in opposition to the value of mysterious wonderment felt by some of the other children, and when these conflicting claims found a resolution in an idea that overarched both. Changes of value are of course part and parcel of changes in personality. In pointing to one, you point to the other.

The Expansion of Personality and Community Through Role-Playing

The entire universe and all the people in time and space are potentially the child's community. But most men grow up recognizing as their own only a small part of the potential community. Many are scarcely even aware of the existence of groups other than their own; and even when this much is accomplished, the individual often is at pains to draw the boundary sharply between whatever he recognizes as his own community and that which he excludes. This rejection of the world can become progressively more exclusive as the individual turns away from men of other nations, of other religions and racial origins; from men of other class status, of other occupations and interests; from men outside his own relatives, even from other than his own immediate family; and finally from others than his own self. Once this point of pathological egocentrism is reached, it is not necessary to take the ultimate step of turning his back upon even himself, for in rejecting the whole of society he has already destroyed himself.

If the child matures in a healthy way, he identifies himself progressively with a wider community, beginning with his mother, father, siblings, relatives, neighborhood friends, and reaching out farther and farther to people of all kinds. No matter where he stops in this process, he suffers at that point arrested development. The race-hater is almost literally still a child tied to his mother's apron strings.

The child who reaches out to the world is building a more adequate self. He looks to his culture for his very mentality. And the more freely he associates with others, the more he has a variety of experiences which he incorporates into his personality. In sharing experiences with people of all kinds he shares their interests, selects from them, and thus broadens and deepens his own range of interests. He selects from society and culture the material which he integrates and reconstructs in the creation of his own personality.

In this process of growing up, role-playing is a key process. The child can identify himself with others by putting himself in their places and seeing what it feels like to face their problems, have their needs, live their lives. Reliving the life of another makes a permanent change in the personality of the child. The other's life becomes a part of his own life; to turn away from the other would be to turn away from himself.

Through role-playing the child not only expands his community but he also finds himself. In coming to know the various roles played in society he finds and creates a role for himself—a role the virtuosity and power of which is in proportion to the opportunities the child has for experimentation with many kinds of roles.

Clearly, then, a task for education is to aid the child in his efforts to experience the roles of others and to find his own role.

In accepting such a responsibility, the school fortunately is in accord with all the natural tendencies of the developing individual. The encouragement of role-playing does not require the injection into the child's life of something strange to his nature. Every healthy child makes growing up his first business, and growing up is largely a matter of learning to manage relations with other human beings more effectively. In its broadest sense, role-playing is at the heart of all the child's consciously directed association with other people. The need to manage these relations creates the need to understand the roles of the others and to understand his own role in relation to theirs. The objective demands of life, not any person, impel the child into role-playing.

Observers of children are nearly all struck by the degree to which dramatic play characterizes their free and uncoerced activity. They learn about the life around them by acting out that life. Their spontaneous play naturally begins with the things close at hand. The child loves to play the parts of father, mother, brother, sister. As the area of his contact with the community broadens, he builds up his repertoire to include the roles of key figures in community life—the bus driver, the milkman, the doctor.

The child's dramatic play includes the characterization of nonhuman and even inanimate objects. He gets down on all fours and becomes an angry, growling animal; hums like an engine and becomes a truck; spreads his arms and becomes an airplane. He builds his understanding of the roles of physical objects in human life by enacting those roles. He is pushing the boundaries of his recognized community out into the physical as well as into the social universe.

In this light, the role-taking of children is seen not as an idiosyncrasy of childhood but as an essential part of the process of growing up. The child is going about the business of understanding the world in which he lives, establishing rapport with it or building a community, and building a self.

Furthermore, role-playing as a natural, spontaneous activity is not limited to childhood. It continues as a major preoccupation of all persons for as long as they continue to mature. There are societies in which overt dramatization plays as important a part in adult life as in child life—for example in Samoa, where both sexes of all ages make dancing a major activity of daily life, and where each develops his own style according to the role he wishes to enact. In our own culture there have been times when we were more spontaneous than today at playing roles—as in the day of the storyteller and the bard, or the day of folk dancing and folk singing. But the inhibitions of contemporary Western life are such that most adults do not overtly enact the roles they play.

Nevertheless, our hunger to play roles is displayed in the eagerness with which we devour the "soap operas" and the true-confession magazines; in the way that we have developed "spectatoritis" in our forms of mass recreation. We want to see what it feels like to live another kind of life than our own. It is to our sorrow that in our culture this vital and natural urge is drained off into fantastic realms rather than channeled into the life of the community where it would help the worker understand the manager, the manager the worker, the Protestant the Jew, the Jew the Catholic, and all to build more adequate selves.

At any rate, the point here being made is that role-playing is a natural tendency both in children and adults, and that the school needs, not to inject a foreign activity, but only to bolster and guide a natural disposition in children, whether they are young or approaching adulthood.

The Stimulation of Role-Playing

There are various ways in which the school can stimulate role-playing. First of all the school needs to help the child become acquainted at firsthand with as much of the life of the community as he can. The child cannot create his roles out of a vacuum; he needs to see, hear, feel, manipulate, the world around him, to come in contact with the varied activities of the community in which he lives.

The following is an example of how firsthand experience led to role-playing, which in turn deepened the meaning of the firsthand experience:

The second-graders had the fun of digging, hoeing, raking, and fertilizing the earth for their garden. They had been thrilled when the first beans pushed up through the soil and spread out their first two leaves to the sun. Now, Karen wondered what it felt like to be down there in the dark soil and to erupt so quickly into the bright sunlight.

"Maybe someone would like to be a seed and show us how it grows," the teacher suggested.

Everyone wanted to volunteer. But Joe had asked first. He stepped out before the circle of chairs occupied by the children and sat with legs crossed, arms folded, and head bent almost to his lap. Very slowly he raised his head, extended his arms, and raised his whole body to standing position. Finally he stood erect with back arched, his arms flung back, and his face turned up to what, he remarked later, was the sun.

Afterwards the children pointed out how well his actions expressed what really happened to the bean, especially in respect to the growth of the two cotyledons.

Then Peter said he could show the way that grass shoots up a single blade. From a position kneeling on one leg he quickly rose while shooting one arm straight into the air. By now other children were clamoring to give their versions of these and other dramatizations about growing things. Some were tried. There was critical discussion of the realism or imaginativeness of each performance, but the teacher took care to keep this within bound so as not spoil the spontaneity and naturalness of the occasion.

Another example, involving older children and more elaborate activity, may be cited:

> The senior class in high-school social studies made a careful study of the election procedure in their community. They visited governmental offices; talked to election officials; visited temporary election booths erected a few days before election day.
>
> In addition, they studied the political issues involved in the campaign itself. They heard speeches; visited and studied a slum area that had figured in the campaigning; analyzed party platforms.
>
> They decided to put on an election of their own, in which they would use all the machinery of official elections, and in which a pre-election campaign would be held. The student candidates and political parties were reproductions of adult prototypes, and they electioneered on the same issues, taking their campaign before the whole school. The mock election was held the day before the actual election.

Other examples are the cooperative planning, building, and operating of grocery stores, post offices, dairies, in the lower grades; or the carrying on of miniature insurance, banking, publishing, or gardening enterprises in the upper grades. Through such activities, which become increasingly varied and complex at higher levels, it is possible for the child to participate imaginatively in basic phases of community life. By being for a number of days a banker, a dairyman, or an insurance agent, the child can understand the respective roles of such persons and extend his concept of community.

Important though firsthand experience may be as a foundation for dramatization, the enormous flexibility and potentiality of role-playing would be missed were its use limited to the re-enactment of what is directly experienced. In fact, the unique advantage of role-playing is that it makes possible the child's participation in activities too remote in time or space to be participated in directly. Although they tended to become conventionalized and thus to lose creativity, some of the standard projects of decades past, in which teachers and children turned their classrooms into reproductions of American Indian, colonial American, or ancient Greek life were on the right track. The following illustrates a less stereotyped approach to the playing of roles remote in time or space.

The seventh-graders were discussing the mysteries involved in the fact that two or more people coming from different places could all manage to meet in a certain spot at a certain time—to find one another in time as well as in space, as it were, though the children did not put it that way. What they wondered about especially was how people managed this feat in the days before watches and clocks existed.

Out of this discussion grew a research project in which several committees investigated methods of telling time used by ancient peoples. After they did some digging around in books they reported to the class, and what they had to tell so fascinated the class that it decided on a further step. This was for each committee to take on the job of reproducing a model of one of the devices on which it had reported.

After several days most of the models were completed, a good deal of research having gone into each one. There was a Chinese water clock, made with large tin cans and wooden floats; a Chinese alarm clock, made with rock weights hanging on strings tied to a horizontally laid punk that could burn; a sundial; and many others, including even a large-scale wooden working model of an escapement mechanism.

Looking over its work, the group decided that these models ought to be good for something more than just looking at. The children finally hit on the idea of writing out a play, one scene to be built around each time-telling device, dramatizing how ancient people might have discovered or invented it.

This required more research. Committees had to find out more about the life and times of each group of people, so that the play could be realistic. While some committees did background research, one committee did research on ancient costumes, and another committee started working out the main action of the play. This last group consulted with the researchers and with the whole class from time to time. Finally the class approved a series of scenes, and dialogue writing was farmed out to some individuals.

As the play worked out, it not only reconstructed possible scenes of antiquity, but it also, coming up to modern times, re-enacted Galileo's famous discovery of the principle of the pendulum. The play helped the children relive some of the experiences of the human race in its search for adequate ways of keeping time.

The concept of role-playing enables us to bring the problem of the teaching of history and geography into better focus. They are subjects which offer the student unusual opportunities to extend the circle bounding his recognized community. History is the record of man's varied occupations and activities from the beginning of recorded time, while geography provides the setting for the study of his occupations and activities all over the world in all sorts of physical environments. What one does vertically the other does horizontally. Between the two of them they give the student access to an enormous amount of human experience extending backward in time and outward in space.

If the child could be helped to relive imaginatively the experience of a great variety of peoples remote in time and space, he would be able to identify himself with a vast community of men—potentially with all men. Having vicariously experienced their values, he would be in a better position to evaluate and test his own.

Perhaps the significance and use of history and geography lie in this. If so, the most promising way to their utilization is suggested. We can regard history, not as a mere chronological record of abstract political events, but rather as the concrete record of living human experiences and activities. Geography is not the study of physical features and political boundaries, but the study of how people make lives for themselves in varied physical settings.

Ultimately, there is probably no better way for children to approach these two resources—geography and history—than through role-playing. At least this is so if they are regarded in the way just suggested. Dates, chronologies, boundaries, descriptions of the world's physical features, might be assimilated without much role-playing. But in themselves they have little meaning. How it felt to live the life of a Greek, the kinds of problems Western pioneers had, what life in China is like today, are matters that require role-playing in order to be understood.

The role-playing need not be as overt as in the case of the children who studied about the ways people told time in the past.

In their case, research into the lives of other people was used as a means for making actual dramatization possible. But children can be helped to experience vicariously without actual dramatization. Anything that helps them project their imaginations into the lives of other people is an aid to role-playing. A simple informal discussion can do this. Talking about what others did, why they did it, how they did it, can stimulate imagination.

Even a child who sits quietly reading about the lives of other people may be taking their roles. In fact, the meaning he grasps probably correlates with the amount and quality of his role-playing. The child who reads mechanically without comprehension is the one whose imagination is not stirred into action as he reads.

Books and other resource materials are indispensable to the child trying to understand the lives of other people. But such resources cannot serve him unless they can somehow fire his imagination. The teacher needs to find ways of helping him relive the scenes being read about. A trip to a museum may acquaint him with the implements, clothing, and housing of the people in whom he is interested. A chance to talk with some person "who was there" may help quicken his imagination. Surrounding him in the classroom with pictures, murals, dioramas, or models made by him or his classmates may help. Classroom discussions in which the children snare their impressions of what it must have felt like to live through the events or in the places being studied should be useful. Recorded music, a poem, a story, may help set a mood or renew a feeling experienced by others who lived in another age or place. But in any case the purpose is the same—to help bring to life an event or an occasion experienced by other persons.

Literature, art, and music perhaps stand beside history and geography as among the most excellent of resources for helping children extend their sense of community through role-playing. These arts go beyond history and geography in that they record, not the unadorned facts of what happened or is happening to people elsewhere, but rather the feelings and responses of these people as they engage in their various activities. Role-playing depends upon being able to have the feelings the other person had.

The arts communicate such feelings directly. Their neglect in the schools can only make the task of breathing life into the study of other people's lives unnecessarily difficult.

Generally speaking, the subject fields mentioned can best make their potentially enormous contribution to the expansion of community if they are not studied for their own sakes in their own separate compartments. The goal is to understand the experiences of other people, not to study geography or art or literature as such. Usually inquiry should start by defining the *kind* of experience that wants to be understood. The children who wanted to know more about the kinds of experiences involved in telling time are a good example. They defined this problem as the study of how people learned to tell time in past ages. Once the problem is defined, it is best to regard the subject fields as resources for solving the problem rather than as organizations of information to be studied for their own sake. Since the children should be free to use any resource regardless of what compartment it happens to be in, the traditional lines of separation between subject fields cannot be maintained. The children studying about time had to use science references in their effort to understand the sundial and the escapement. They had to use history references in order to understand how people came upon these discoveries. They had to use geography references to understand how it was that physical surroundings made Egyptians look to the sun as a teller of time while South Sea Islanders looked to dripping water for the same thing. Literature and art helped make the human response to these events clearer.

In short, the sense of community can expand best when human experience is taken as the unit to be studied, and when subject fields serve primarily as resources for stimulating either vicarious or overt re-enactment of such experiences.

Role-Playing in the Creative Social Act

The examples in the foregoing pages represent role-playing as the more or less conscious focus of effort. There is another and more profound sense, however, in which role-playing can be encouraged by the school.

This is role-playing as the normal characteristic of the daily activities and occupations of the children. The more children are brought into participative relationship with one another and with their physical and social environment, the more the natural role-playing of everyday life is promoted. Every cooperative act entails role-playing as its necessary accompaniment. Coordination, division of labor, timing, are practical problems which can be solved only as the participants understand the roles of one another in the common enterprise. As one directs his own act, he must also internally and in his imagination act out the roles of others with whom his actions are to integrate.

Consequently, the method par excellence of promoting role-playing among children is to make cooperative problem-solving—the creative social act—the basic feature of school life. It is possible to be specific about the ways in which role-playing is called out in the children as they seek cooperatively to attack common problems.

In the first place, to recall a point made previously, the determination of a common problem requires role-playing. The conflicting value claims of the children can be resolved by their seeking a community of experience upon which to base their value judgments. The teacher can help by promoting an atmosphere for objective discussion. In such a setting the children can show one another the experiences upon which they base their respective claims. The teacher can help the children "get inside" one another's experience by aiding each participant in his effort to communicate effectively. He can make suggestions which point toward possible ways of integrating conflicting claims.

In the second place, policy having been agreed upon, role-playing is demanded of the children by the need cooperatively to plan and organize their work. Cooperative work calls for different parts to be carried out by each participant. These various roles must be planned by the group and provided for in the assigning of personnel. The group must determine what these various roles are to be—some children are to do research, some to arrange excursions, some to produce charts or models, for example. The group must define each of these roles specifically enough so that the individuals assigned to them know what is expected of them, but not so specifically as to hinder any individual's originality and creativity. As the group concentrates on the planning of a given role, it is, for the moment, in imagination living that role.

Third, the execution of the plan requires continual role-playing. Each worker must put himself in the place of each other person with whom he seeks to correlate his actions. At the simplest level, this is illustrated by two boys sawing a board. The one holding the board must internally do the sawing, too, if his board holding is to be done in a way that satisfies the requirements of the sawyer. When co-workers become irritated with one another, the reason often is the feeling on the part of one that the other shows insufficient imagination in anticipating the first one's actions and adjusting to them. Or the trouble may be that one party to the cooperative act expects the other to be alert in anticipating his acts, but is not willing in return to exercise the same alertness. Such incidents are evidence of breakdown in the role-playing process, and afford the teacher the opportunity to help the children analyze the situation and see their mutual role-playing obligations.

And finally, the children's evaluation of a common activity following its culmination brings out role-playing. If evaluation is done in a group-discussion situation, each child has a personal reaction to communicate to the others. He feels a certain way about the recently completed activity, and his job is to help others feel what he feels. Their job in turn is to put themselves in his place and to see things at least for a moment as he does. Through this process the children can move toward a degree of common feeling about the value of what they have just done and a common persuasion as to improvements in future activities. Perhaps it is in this final role-playing that a group concluding a successful activity can achieve its deepest feeling of fellowship and community. The members now have an experience in common which binds them together and in which they may take deep satisfaction.

Such high points in the experiences of children should not be allowed to be forgotten. As a group moves on to other activities, occasions should be set aside for the recall and enjoyment of the high lights of previous common experiences. A group that has done things successfully has a community of memory, and time should be provided for the commemoration and celebration of this fact. An evening at a teacher's home, class parties on the last day of school—any occasion capable of an atmosphere conducive to feelings of communion—can be used for this purpose.

The child deserves a life in school in which he can find both fellowship and an adequate personal role within the life of the group. He deserves such experiences, not only for the inherent satisfaction in them, but equally because they help build in him a character which is disposed to reach out to other persons and which is skilled in the art of relating to others, rather than a character which is disposed to turn inward and become exclusive. The child's power to expand continuously the boundaries of his recognized community and to find therein a growing self will enable him to break through many of the limitations that might otherwise restrict his sense of community and his feeling of individuality.[2]

[2] No discussion of role-playing should end without at least a reference to the experimentation with psychodrama and sociodrama which is being done by various groups throughout the country. This development is a stimulating and promising effort to study in a systematic way what happens when participants in a common enterprise internalize the roles of one another, and to work out tested and specific techniques by which the individual can be helped to understand both others and himself better by internalizing the roles of others. There has already been some effort—and it is to be hoped there will be more—to apply these techniques in public-school classrooms.

As with so many once-promising developments in education, there is some danger that sociodrama and psychodrama may not, as their development in the schools continues, be seen in proper perspective. They are essentially techniques, part of a larger process. As techniques, they should not take the place of the whole process itself. In the discussion above, an effort has been made to show role-playing as an inherent part of the total process of cooperative problem-solving. If role-playing is kept in this, its proper context, and if psychodrama and sociodrama are seen as special techniques within a larger context, then they should realize their potentialities.

For treatment of sociodrama as applied to education, see Helen Hall Jennings, "Sociodrama as Educative Process," *Fostering Mental Health in Our Schools* (Washington, D. C.: Association for Supervision and Curriculum Development, 1950 yearbook, pp. 260-285); and Robert B. Haas, editor, *Psychodrama and Sociodrama in American Education* (New York: Beacon House, 1940).

CHAPTER VIII

The Executive Mode

THE religious individual mobilizes his resources and energies for the purpose of contributing to the realization of the ideal values to which he is dedicated. His behavior is distinguished from the aimless drifting, the undirected fits and starts, the half-hearted temporizing, of those persons who lack dedication to an ideal. This getting things done, this carrying out or executing the basic commitments of life, may be designated as the executive mode.

A glance at the history of Christianity may seem to invalidate the claim that religion has executive quality. The militant aggressiveness of the Salvation Army and of the "social gospel" may not seem typical. Has not Christianity had a history of withdrawal into monasteries, of passive acceptance of existing social arrangements, and even of active collaboration with ruling forces in society interested in preserving the *status quo*? Instead of working to transform the world for the better, has not religion, as the Marxists say, been the opiate of the people?

The present thesis is that there is discernible in religion *both* an acquiescent and an executive mode, and that these two are complementary to one another rather than mutually exclusive.

The acquiescent mode appears historically in two forms: acquiescence to the prevailing social order by withdrawal from it, and acquiescence to the prevailing order by acceptance of and involvement in it. Withdrawal from the world was the dominant mode of early Christianity; acceptance of the existing order the dominant mode of the medieval Church.

Both forms of acquiescence were challenged by the rise of the modern aggressive sects, with their tendency to transform the world through action aimed at the religious ideal. The aggressive sects illustrate Christianity in the executive mode. Consideration of these developments in Christianity will help throw light upon the relations of the executive and acquiescent modes in religion.

Acquiescence in Early Christianity and in the Medieval Church

The peoples of the ancient world, crushed by oppression, social struggles, and the collapse of the forces with which they identified their respective civilizations, tended to withdraw from the external world and find salvation in an inner spiritual world. It was in this atmosphere that Christianity was born.

It appeared to men living in this age that the social ideal could not be realized by human thought and effort. The psychological reaction was the renunciation both of the temporal order and of the idea that it could be transformed through material, political, social, or economic means.

Instead there was a turning to the inward treasures of peace of mind, love of humanity, and fellowship with God. These values were discoverable by all in their own hearts. The attitude toward the external world became one of patience, endurance, and long-suffering forbearance.

The accepted doctrine of early Christianity, serving both to explain this state of affairs and to answer the argument of any Christian who wished to take part in secular life, was formulated as follows: The social order is the result of man's sin. By participating in it the Christian submits to the sin of humanity. Externally he must submit, but in his heart he is still opposed. At least he finds no inner pleasure when he submits.

The second type of acquiescence—through acceptance of the existing social order—was manifested in the medieval Church.

A distinction made by Ernst Troeltsch[1] helps show the meaning of this. Troeltsch is able to discern throughout the history of Christianity the continuous development of two sociological religious types—the church-type and the sect-type.

The essential characteristic of the sect-type is that it rejects the prevailing social arrangements and modes of life and formulates instead an ethos which it believes to be more rigorously moral than that which prevails. In doing this it becomes hostile to the community and incurs the hostility of the community in turn; it shatters the community.

An essential characteristic of the church-type, in contrast, is its desire not to shatter but to preserve the community. The church-type may have an ethos that differs from that of the community as much as does that of the sect-type; but in the church-type's anxiety to preserve the community it first compromises with and then accepts the prevailing secular order. At the same time, however, it seeks to extend its dominion over the community in order to preserve the organic relations of the latter intact. Whereas the sect-type consists of individuals who come together voluntarily to share a vision they hold in common, the church-type declares its sovereignty over all members of society.

For the sect-type there exists only absolute law, which is taken to be ordained by God and which embodies the ethos of the group. It is rigid adherence to the law which severs the sect from the community at large, since the latter lives by the opposed and false law manifested in the prevailing customs of the sinful world. The church-type, in contrast, makes its compromise with the temporal order by declaring the existence of two realms of law. In addition to the absolute law of God there exists the relative law observable in the temporal order, which is regarded as a stepping-stone to the realization of the absolute law. In this way the church is able to accept society as it is and to regard the present order, however apparent its evil, as part of the divine plan for salvation.

Hence the church-type tends to be tolerant and forgiving of the

[1] Ernst Troeltsch, *The Social Teaching of the Christian Churches.*

weaknesses and sin of men, and to devote its energies to softening the evils of the existing social system without transforming the system itself.

Thus the medieval Church saw the hierarchical social system of feudalism as part of the divine plan. Feudal society was seen as an organism in which each class had its part to play. The duty of each man was to accept his assigned role in society and to fulfil it with proper regard to the prospering of the whole. Rulers and ruled, guardians and workers, there must be, but the responsibility of the rulers included concern for the welfare of the workers as well as for their governance.

The Church was not insensitive to the human misery associated with the feudal system and sought to alleviate it through emphasis upon the ideal of charity in human association. The aim was not to transform society but to improve the lot of men within existing arrangements through a spirit of charitable kindness in the relations of men and through widespread philanthropic activity.

Yet because of the ease with which the need for universal community became confused with the Church's compulsion to extend its power over every individual and over all aspects of life, the Church was blind to the evils that resulted from the concentration of power in the hands of a few, was capable of the barbaric savagery of the Inquisition, could sanctify war if it was of a kind that seemed advantageous to the Church, and could stand in the way of the advancement of human knowledge when the latter appeared to challenge its doctrine.

The Revolutionary Effect of Sect-Type Acquiescence

In contrast to the church-type's acquiescence, the sect-type sometimes tends to display the militant spirit which, conscious of the evils of the social order, seeks to transform it fundamentally. It must be pointed out at the start, however, that the sect-type may and does occur in history as an acquiescent type as well as an executive type. The common element in either case which distinguishes the sect from the church is rejection of, hostility toward, and withdrawal from the prevailing order. But in its withdrawal the sect may become either quietistic or aggressive.

On the one hand, it may be satisfied to work out a reformed social arrangement only in its limited community while tending to ignore the rest of the world, as in the case, for example, of the early Quakers.[2] On the other hand the withdrawn sect may feel a compulsion to extend the social transformation it achieves within itself to the entire community. The sect then returns to the world as an aggressive group seeking to revolutionize the world. Examples are the Anabaptists and the left wing of Unitarianism.

Before the role of the aggressive sect is considered, it will prove helpful to mention certain sociological functions of the quietistic sect. The role of the quietistic sect may be characterized as one of withdrawn but quiet effectiveness which without intending to, does in fact transform the social order as radically as any social force known. Even though this effect is not intended, it is no accident but a logical result of the nature of the sect-type.

The three most prominent examples that may be offered are the original Christian sectarianism of Jesus, the essentially sectarian spirit of monasticism, and the role of the mystical and quietistic sect-type in the development of modern democracy.

The argument as to whether the message of Jesus was a program of social reform or not is perhaps based on the failure of both sides to distinguish between the nonrevolutionary intent and the revolutionary effect of the Gospel. The Gospel was not a call for social reform but a summons to prepare for the Kingdom of God. This preparation was to take place quietly within the framework of the present world order, yet in a withdrawn attitude from that order. There was to be a fellowship of love among those who, living within the world, nevertheless rejected it. Preparation consisted of conquering the self, not society, which could only be submitted

[2] This does not mean, of course, that the quietistic sect does not expect a transformed world. The issue is one of *how* the world is to be transformed—through God-inspired but humanistic action, or through passive resistance, the ultimate outcome being primarily or even solely in the hands of God.

to in humility. That must be rendered unto Caesar which he demanded, but Caesar had no control over the Christian's heart. Jesus' injunctions about wealth were not a call to the overthrowing of wealth but simply the pointing out of the handicap that the possession of wealth placed upon the individual effort to transform the heart.

But despite the quietism of Jesus and his followers, the long-term effect of their activities was revolutionary. The refusal to be spiritually cowed by existing conditions struck a responsive chord in the masses of men and resulted in passive but decisive rejection of the ethics upon which Roman rule was based. The outcome was the penetration of Rome itself by Christianity, and eventually the ascendancy of the Church over the state. The once-persecuted Christians came to occupy the seats of the mighty.

Monasticism's influence upon civilization was no less great. Monasticism is an example of sectarian spirit within the Church. When it is pointed out that monasticism was essentially a protest against the worldliness of the Church, its sectarian quality is indicated. The monastic group, like all sectarian groups, was a relatively small community which, rejecting the world, withdrew from it in order to lead its own transformed life upon the basis of love. It was no accident that the heresies of Christendom were born in the monasteries. The contrast between the monk's renunciation of worldly goods and the Church's wealth and power epitomizes the contrast between monasticism's rejection of the temporal order and the Church's acceptance of it.

Monasticism was sectarianism of the quietistic type, yet its influence upon the world was enormous and in the end revolutionary. Throughout the Middle Ages monasticism was the guardian of the Western world's culture—its learning, literature, art, and science. It is sufficient to point to the latter—science—to suggest the extent to which monasticism prepared the way and helped make possible the release of creative energy that began with the Renaissance. It was from the laboratories of the monasteries that Roger Bacon emerged to confront intellectual authoritarianism with the challenge of the experimental conception of the nature of science. In contrast it was the Church, not the monasteries, which sought to suppress the revolutionary discoveries and experimental method of Galileo.

The relation of mysticism to the modern development of democracy provides a third example of the ultimately revolutionary effect of the quietistic sect-type.[3] Mysticism is based on faith in the possibility of direct inward and present religious experience. Hence it is highly individualistic and finds much in common with the sect-type insistence that religion is a direct affair between the devotee and God without the mediation of the priesthood. Wherever the sect-type and mysticism are joined there is found a belief in the universal priesthood of the worshipers, in the equality of all men before God, and in the freedom of the individual to interpret his own religious experience.

In accordance with such beliefs, mystical sectarian groups tend toward the congregational type of religious organization, with its democratic and equalitarian traits. They have engaged in such experiments as the practice of communism within their own group. One quietistic mystical sect, the Quakers, has developed techniques for determining policy through voluntary consensus. The great upsurge of both sectarianism and mysticism in the seventeenth century helped create in England a ferment of democratic ideas which had a profound influence upon Western civilization. Men who had experienced democracy in their religious life were likely to expect and demand it in political life as well.

Executive Quality in the Aggressive Sect-Type

The revolutionary effects of the quietistic sect-type are unpremeditated and not intended. But in turning to the modern aggressive sect-type, one encounters the existence of conscious reforming intent.

[3] See Rufus Jones, *Mysticism and Democracy in the English Commonwealth*, and Troeltsch, *op. cit.*, II, pp. 691-800.

Each of the three major examples of the church-type in Christianity—Catholicism, Lutheranism, and Calvinism—has been responsible for conditions which created its own constellation of aggressive sects. The medieval Church was related to, notably, the socially and religiously revolutionary groups which first appeared in the fourteenth and fifteenth centuries under the leadership of John Wyclif and John Huss, and which became known by such names as Lollards and Hussites. The two Protestant churches, with Calvinism predominant, were related to the appearance of the modern aggressive sects, which include such groups as the Anabaptists, the radical Baptists, the Levelers, the Diggers, the Unitarians, the American Humanist Societies, and the Ethical Culture Societies.

There have been several efflorescences of aggressive sectarianism in modern times. One occurred in the seventeenth century and played a great part in the English Revolution. Another occurred in the Evangelical Revival of the eighteenth century, at which time such men as John and Charles Wesley and William Wilberforce led large numbers of Methodists and Anglicans in crusades for social and political reform.

The aggressive sect rejects the prevailing order as representing a state of affairs resulting from sin. But unlike the quietistic sect it believes that the present world must be the means to a better world. The Kingdom of God is not an ideal social order unrelated to present existence, but rather is the result of the transformation of present existence. The aggressive sect usually recognizes the close connection of spiritual and material aspects of life. It is determined to understand and use the material world in the realization of the spiritual world. In this sense the aggressive sect accepts the world, even though it is hostile to it. Acceptance is coupled with the demand that the world's sinful aspects be overcome. Sin is to be overcome not through individual effort alone but through reconstruction of the social order in such a way that the individual's environment encourages his morality.

Executive-Acquiescent Synthesis in Calvinism

Calvinism represents in the history of Christianity a new sociological type, in which are combined the conservatism and organicism of the church-type with the progressivism and individualism of the aggressive sect-type.[4] On the one hand there are Calvinism's conscious impulse toward expansion, its power to form large, strong ecclesiastical organizations, and its tendency to penetrate the political and economic life of the world. These are characteristic traits of the church-type. On the other hand there are Calvinism's tendency to uphold a religious ideal against which the present order is measured, and Calvinism's promotion of independent individualism in its devotee. These are characteristic traits of the sect-type.

Calvin did not conceive the Church as merely the objective means of grace by virtue of whose existence the world's ungodliness may be accepted. The Church should be the instrument of God's will, not merely the vehicle of his grace. It should be active in Christianizing the community by bringing the whole range of life under the control of Christian regulations and purposes. Here was a church-type organicism which was both conservative and radical. The Church, conceived in this way, remained within and was coexistent with society, and yet was able to criticize it. Its criticism could point beyond the mere Christianizing of human relations within existing social arrangements to improvements of the arrangements themselves.

At the same time Calvinist individualism provided an additional challenge to society, and brought to Calvinism a certain affinity with the sect-type. In defining the religious responsibility of the individual, Calvinism joined with Lutheranism in rejecting the Catholic emphasis upon good works. Instead, both insisted upon the doctrine of justification by faith. Catholicism, as Pharisaism before it, had tended to identify good works with the mere observance of external formalities, such as fasting, prayer, and almsgiving.

[4] *Ibid.*, II, pp. 576-623.

The two Protestant churches, like the prophets and Jesus before them, called instead for a complete change of heart. But it was Calvinism which especially emphasized the fact that the result and test of a change of heart is behavior itself. The dedication of every daily act to one's religious ideal is the real test of faith.

The Calvinist doctrine of predestination placed a peculiar imperative upon its demand for action. The Calvinist knew not only that his Calling and election were sure but also that he was in virtue of this a particularly distinguished member of society. He felt an obligation to fulfil his divinely appointed mission in life. The fact that his failure to do so would be prima facie evidence that he was not after all of the elect perhaps increased the demand he felt. In any case, the individual was drawn into a wholehearted absorption in unceasing, rigorous labor.

The effect upon him was, paradoxically, to make him independent of the Church. Ultimately the realization of his salvation became a personal matter between him and God; thus his religious spirit developed an affinity with the individualism of the sect-type.

The Social Gospel in America

The degree to which Calvinism has influenced the peculiar culture that has developed in the United States of America has never been determined with any precision. It is plain that its influence has been great, and that Calvinism-Puritanism-Baptism-aggressive sectarianism form a complex of related elements which have penetrated American life deeply.[5] Regardless of the degree to which Calvinism may or may not have contributed to it, activism has been a notable characteristic of American Christianity.

One of the conspicuous features of American organized religion has been its spirit of social reform.[6] This flowered in the late nine-

[5] Ralph Barton Perry, *Puritanism and Democracy*, has analyzed the relationship between one of these elements, Puritanism, and the American democratic tradition.

[6] See Winfred E. Garrison, "Characteristics of American Organized Religion," *Annals of the American Academy of Political and Social Science*, March, 1948,

teenth and early twentieth centuries under the slogan of the "social gospel." It was during this era that Walter Rauschenbusch developed and spread the credo which has since constituted a bulwark of what has become the social-gospel tradition.[7] This credo included the principles that the development of human beings, not the accumulation of wealth and power, should be the purpose of economic activity; that human rights should prevail over property rights; that socioeconomic planning must replace the struggle for profit.

In this same period the idea that Christianity and socioeconomic reconstruction are closely related was popularized by Edward Bellamy's *Looking Backward* (1867), which was only one of a number of similar best-selling works.

The social gospel has not been confined to a few radical sects, but has instead made its presence felt in nearly every important religious body in America, including Judaism and Catholicism as well as the Protestant denominations. Nearly every one of these groups has set up numerous commissions and committees concerned with social and economic problems. In nearly every case the pronouncements of these committees have followed the direction of Rauschenbusch's thinking.

The Federal Council of Churches of Christ, representing most of the important Protestant denominations, was organized within a year of the publication of *Christianity and the Social Crisis*. It issued at once its first pronouncement, the "Social Creed of the Churches," which followed the Rauschenbusch pattern, and which has set the tone of the influential activities of the Council to this date. Similar pronouncements have come from Judaism and Catholicism. This common ground was most decisively expressed in 1946 when the Synagogue Council of America, the Industrial Relations Division of the Federal Council of Churches of Christ, and the

pp. 14-24. Also, in the same volume, see John Herman Randall, "The Churches and the Liberal Tradition," pp. 148-164; Hanly Furfey, "The Churches and Social Problems," pp. 101-109; and Harry F. Ward, "Organized Religion, the State, and the Economic Order," pp. 72-83.

[7] This credo is stated in Rauschenbusch's *Christianity and the Social Crisis*.

Social Action Department of the National Catholic Welfare Conference released jointly a "Declaration on Economic Justice," which, whether the signers realized it or not, closely followed the Rauschenbusch program.

It is true that the emphasis on social action in American religion often does not get far beyond the resolution-passing stage. While the large religious groups have within the last fifteen years become interested in Christian social action to the extent that nearly all of them have set up national organizations and staffs for this purpose, this type of organization is ineffective in most cases. For example, one of the largest denominations, with 4,000,000 members, had in 1946 a national social-action organization staffed by two part-time workers on $1,000 budget.[8]

Nevertheless, the vigor and effectiveness of the social gospel in America cannot be minimized. The pronouncements of the Federal Council of Churches are taken seriously by the members of Congress. The theological seminaries, the social consciousness of whose staffs is reputed to be exceeded by the faculties of no other form of higher education in the nation, are turning out a new generation of activist-minded clergymen. The socially progressive writings of Reinhold Niebuhr, Harry F. Ward, E. B. Chaffee, C. M. Morrison, Walter M. Horton, John C. Bennett, A. J. Muste, and many others continue to influence the nation.

The Meaning of Execution and Acquiescence in Religion

What interpretation of the meaning of the executive mode in religious experience can be drawn from the material just sketched?

The executive mode consists of active participation in the practical affairs of life in a way that transforms existence in the direction of a more ideal state of affairs.

But there exists also another mode—one of acquiescence to the unsatisfactory state of existence. This may take either of two forms

[8] Judson T. Landis, "Social Action and American Protestant Churches," *American Journal of Sociology*, May, 1947, pp. 517-522.

—acquiescence by submission to and participation in the existing order, or acquiescence by withdrawal into a voluntary community that quietly lives apart from the rest of the world.

It is possible to resolve the apparent contradiction between execution and acquiescence. First we must identify what is valid in each.

The great contribution of the executive mode is its bringing of present and desired states of existence into relationship with one another. In this mode there is recognition of the fact that the existing state of affairs, no matter how evil it may be, is the material that needs to be worked with and reconstructed.

In doing this the executive mode brings means and ends into relation with one another. There is willingness to formulate practical rather than absolute ends because it is recognized that present conditions determine the goals attainable in the foreseeable future.

There appears in the executive mode an imperative to action that does not appear when utopias are separated from the means of their attainment. The formulation of ends in terms of available materials and existing conditions means that the process of determining goals also determines the steps by which they are attainable. The psychological result is readiness for action—a tendency to move ahead because there are envisioned both a desired outcome and the way to its achievement.

What, in comparison, are the strong features of the acquiescent mode?

First, acquiescence of the church-type suggests that acceptance of the world is the necessary prelude to its transformation. It is a common observation that he who would be influential in the world must be a part of the world, not apart from it. The reformer who has the greatest impact upon a community is often the one who is felt by the community to be one of its own members.

Acceptance of the community by the reformer preserves the lines of communication between the reformer and the community. The way in which this operates can be stated in terms of organization for action. The achievement of a more ideal state of affairs by a group calls for a certain degree of coordinated organization within the group. The larger the group, the more complex the problem of organization becomes. The function of the leaders of an organization includes the establishing and maintaining of lines of communication and central clearing points of communication.[9]

This is true even of an authoritarian type of organization, such as an army in the field, in which general headquarters serves as the center of communication. But the communicative function becomes increasingly and even more essentially the function of leadership as the organization becomes more democratic in character, since the formulation of policy is a concern of all the individuals involved. Organization establishes a number of channels which aid communication because they are recognized by the participants as regularly available means of intercourse.

But astute leaders of organizations know that the establishment of formal lines of communication is not in itself enough to insure effectiveness. Organizations fail unless they also have a well-established informal organization. Informal organization is created in the personal relations among the participants. It lacks formal structure, arising as it does from contacts which may be incidental to more formally organized activities, from gregarious tendencies, or from social interactions which may have no purpose beyond the satisfactions that accrue from participation with sympathetic and like-minded people. Yet man, in his political moods, recognizes the critical importance of informal organization in affecting the experiences, attitudes, emotions, and knowledge of the persons concerned. Customs, mores, folkways, and many of our social norms have been created more through informal organization than through the formal organization of society.

When formal organization degenerates into formality for its own sake, it either cramps action unnecessarily or else it becomes a mere decoration superimposed on the informal organization which does

[9] This conception of the executive function has been put forward by Chester I. Barnard, *The Function of the Executive*. See especially pp. 114-126 and 217-226.

the real work. When formal organization becomes separated from informal organization, the latter becomes dominated by unavowed and nonpublic interests and vested minorities. If formal and informal organizations are kept in proper relation to one another, the former supplements the latter in exposing the full scope of interests to publicity and scrutiny by the participants.

The individuals and groups who would be effective in transforming society have an advantage if they are sufficiently a part of society to be able to take part in its informal organization. Effective formal organization for action is built upon an established informal organization and creates new informal organizational arrangements. Unless the reformer or leader accepts the group and is accepted by it, he finds it impossible to participate in informal organization. This is the essential truth which seems to be recognized by the church-type of acquiescence. The danger is that in becoming involved in the community, one may surrender to it. Yet it appears that this is a risk which needs to be run.

The world has witnessed in Russian communism an example of what happens to the executive mode when it is insufficiently supplemented by church-type acquiescence. In its doctrine of class conflict, communist theory embraces the strategy of the shattered community as a means of achieving the ideally transformed society. But to shatter the community by rejecting elements of it, while in turn being rejected by these same elements, is to create a situation in which an increasingly greater premium must be placed upon coercive power. The reforming sect is either driven to the use of coercion, with corrupting results, or, ignored by the hostile community, the sect becomes ineffectual as a moral force in the world. The revolutionary who loves the world and whom the world loves is clearly much more effective in reforming it.

There appear to be several instructive strategies of action manifested in quietistic sectarian behavior.

Quietism displays practical realism combined with devoted idealism when it recognizes that the reformer cannot always bend the world to his will and yet that the reformer must not succumb to the world. Even in the face of overwhelming odds and an implacable universe the individual may still maintain an inner integrity and sense of responsibility. Faced by a situation to which less committed individuals and groups might succumb, the quietest retires, as an individual, into himself or, as a member of a sect, into a restricted community, there to cultivate the ideal which might otherwise be lost to the world. This ideal can return to contribute riches to the world when the world becomes more favorably disposed to accept them, as is demonstrated by the history of monasticism.

Quietism insists that nothing less than a complete change of heart is sufficient to the moral growth of the individual. Mere externalities of action are not sufficient evidence of the existence of good will. The moral regeneration of the whole personality is required.

How is a change of heart produced? One might point to the failure of some participants in the American acquisitive economy to change their ethical outlook and to place economic life on a higher moral plane. The failure is in part due to the fact that the system breeds its own immorality. The argument between those who would transform our socioeconomic life by first transforming the morals of men, and those who would transform the morals of men by first transforming the economy, rests upon an implied separation of the acquiescent and executive modes. If in the quietistic mode men can achieve a change of heart while simultaneously in the executive mode transforming the conditions that change the heart, there is a better chance that morality and objective social arrangements will strengthen one another and progress together in reciprocal stimulation.

Execution and Acquiescence in the Creative Social Act

The paradox involved in the existence of both executive and acquiescent conduct in religious life is perhaps resolvable in terms of the creative social act.

The individual in the executive mode enters the creative social act fired with the vision of an ideal and the determination to contribute to its realization. But in the acquiescent mode he realizes that the workings of the social act surpass his understanding and that he can only surrender himself to it. Are not both modes essential to the social act? The creative social act lives on the individual contributions made to it. Yet creativity is destroyed if anyone tries to take command of the social act on the assumption that his insights are better than those that can emerge from the participating group.

The church- and sect-types of acquiescence are respectively two different ways of surrendering to the creative social act.[10]

Church-type acquiescence accepts the world because it has faith in the future of the world, even though it cannot know what that future may be. This acquiescence sees the present state of the world as the material out of which a better world will develop. It seeks to know this material intimately, to involve itself in it, and thereby to establish a community and a basis for working with the world.

Sectarian acquiescence, on the other hand, withdraws from the world in order to cultivate the creative social act in the seclusion of a limited community.

Each type of acquiescence complements the other. The creativity of a withdrawn group produces contributions to society which are deviant, varied, and stimulating. Society profits by having a variety of such contributions from which to select. But at the same time

[10] The question of whether, historically, acquiescence led to action through strategic intent or accident is answerable in the following way:

Acquiescence placed the outcome of life's struggles in the hands of God. This is the metaphorical way of expressing surrender to the creative social act. Hence none of the changes wrought by acquiescence could have been strategically intended. But neither were they accidents. Acquiescence was based on the faith that through God's grace *some* kind of improvement in existence would be forthcoming. What was required of man was purity of heart—his cultivation of the highest ideals he could conceive, even though he could not know how nor in what form they would be realized. Undoubtedly the effort to become pure in heart resulted in acquiescence having a different effect upon the world than would have been the case if "acquiescence" had meant a mere surrender to brute impulses.

there must be forces in society which tend to integrate and unify the varied contributions of special groups. There must be the kind of acquiescence which surrenders to the ultimate creative social act in which all humanity participates. Sectarian and churchly acquiescence contribute respectively to valuational differentiation and valuational integration.

The executive and acquiescent modes need one another. Either one without the other destroys creativity. Execution without acquiescence takes its ideals and ways of working as final. In refusing to submit to the transforming power of the creative social act, such execution rejects the contributions of others. But acquiescence without execution is impotent. Even though the whole world with all its sin may be taken to one's bosom without a censorious attitude, to change the world is still desirable. One may love all men as personalities, yet still wish to cast out the evil in their behavior.

CHAPTER IX

The Executive Mode: Education

Developing Strength of Character

EDUCATION for religious quality in experience should build into the characters of children the power to mobilize and organize their life energies for the realiziation of the growing body of ideal value to which they become committed. The ability to act decisively, effectively, and courageously in behalf of tested ideals is the ultimate test of religious devotion to them.

Such strength and discipline of character must be distinguished from the arrogant conduct which is based on the assumption of exclusive accessibility to the right ideal and the right way of attaining it. Religious strength of character includes humility, which recognizes one's inevitable fallibility and submits to the corrective process of group thinking and cooperative action.

The development of executive quality in conduct is the equivalent of what in the past has often been thought of as the development of the will. Accordingly it should prove profitable to consider this older idea of the will and its relation to what is here conceived as executive quality in conduct.

The ancient controversy over the question of freedom of the will is based upon an assumption held in common by both parties to the controversy. The will is assumed to be a private possession of the individual over which he exerts ultimate control. Those who base their belief in freedom of the will upon this assumption hold the individual personally and exclusively accountable for his acts. They usually recognize that environing factors have an enormous influence upon the individual. But they think in terms of an individual who succumbs or does not succumb to these influences, depending upon his strength of will. Will is seen as separated from and inherently opposed to the environment. Any agreement between the respective directions in which the will and the environment impel one is simply a fortunate accident. Typically, the individual accomplishes his duties in spite of, not because of, the invitations which the environment extends to him.

Absolute determinism, on the other hand, holds that every act of the individual is completely out of his hands and is determined by the outside forces acting upon him. The determinists have an undeniable point when they insist upon the enormous influence of environment on behavior. Realizing this, they see that an autonomous and completely private will can be no more than an absolute fiction. Assuming that this is the only way to conceive will, they deny the existence of will altogether.

The ordinary man with his good common sense knows that he does have some control of his acts, but that he is controlled also by the forces that surround him. The argument about free will strikes him as a metaphysical subtlety unworthy of the attention of practical men. But the trouble is that this debate, whether it is a cause or a result, is related to basic practices in our culture which profoundly affect the life of the individual. These practices enter the schools and there influence our children for better or worse.

The outmoded faculty psychology included the will with other faculties which, like muscles, could be developed by appropriate exercises. Faculty psychology implicitly assumed the doctrine of free will. Though as a psychological theory this view is dead, the practices it upheld are still all too prevalent in the schools. Being in command of a private possession or faculty known as the will, the child is expected to exercise that faculty. It is expected of the child that, knowing his duty, he shall exert his will to perform it. The school's primary responsibility, then, is to acquaint him with his duty. The rest is up to him. Accordingly, verbal instruction, exhortation, inculcation, catechizing, become the stand-bys used by the school in what is known as the training of character. Insofar as the school assumes responsibility at all for creating environmental conditions which actually produce executive conduct, it tends to see this responsibility in terms of making work hard for children. Any task that is sufficiently difficult exercises the faculty of will. A premium is even placed upon unpleasantness—an unpleasant task challenges the will as no pleasant one can.

A different tack is taken by the determinists in education. Their method is epitomized in the statement of the behaviorist J. B. Watson:

> No matter how many thousands of reactions a human or animal is capable of performing, there is always some stimulus or object in the environment which will arouse each of these reactions in him. Our search in the laboratory at the present time lies in this direction, to get a better knowledge of the stimuli calling out reactions. With this data well in hand, it is a simple enough matter then to arrange the environment, put the necessary group of stimuli in front of him, to get man or animal to perform any act in his repertoire. . . . We hope to reach such proficiency in our science that we can build any man, starting at birth, into any kind of social or a-social being upon order.[1]

According to this view, behavior is absolutely determined by environing conditions. The purpose or the will of the individual can be of no account in determining what he does. Will and purpose may be present, but if so they are the products of environing circumstances, which thus remain the ultimate causative agents.

The alternative to conceiving will as the private possession of the individual is to regard it as a function of the relation between individual and environment. There are forces *both* in the environment and internal to the individual which, in acting and reacting upon one another, determine behavior. The individual is not seen as absolutely sovereign in determining his own behavior. His purposed behavior may have its impact upon the environment, but

[1] J. B. Watson, *The Ways of Behaviorism* (New York: Harper & Brothers, 1928, pp. 17-20). Reprinted by permission.

the response of the environment in turn changes his purposes. But while he is not sovereign, still his intelligent choices do count for something. He is not plastic material molded by his environment, but an organization of energy which not only responds to the environment but also, in responding, changes the environment.

This view seems to harmonize better with the facts of religious experience than does either a one-sided voluntaristic or deterministic view. It does justice to the religious feeling that God's grace "abounds in man"; that an infinite intelligence and power manifest themselves finitely in the behavior of men. This idea was never intended to mean that man was not responsible for his own acts. It does mean that any given act is the product of forces which *in their totality* are beyond the control and comprehension of man. But within the total field of energy there is one center of energy, man himself, over which man does have some control. He can control *some* of the energy that contributes to a given act, yet the final outcome is a resolution of forces beyond his control.

The development of executive quality in behavior, then, is achieved neither by exhortation, which puts responsibility for conduct upon the child alone, nor by environmental manipulation, which removes all personal responsibility.

Instead, executive quality is developed when the child has opportunity to assume responsibility for carrying out his own intelligently made choices. When it is recognized that his conduct is a resolution of environmental and personal forces, he is dealt with accordingly. He is held accountable, but not to a rigid standard of behavior which takes no account of circumstances and conditions. What motivates him—what gives his acts the power and force that we associate with "will power"—is not his rigid adherence to an arbitrary standard of "duty" but rather his own insight into the inherent demands of a situation.

True, his insight will be immeasurably aided if he is acquainted with the standards by which the human race judges situations. The school must help him know and understand such standards. But the demands of a given situation are unique and particular to that situation. They are biological and psychological as well as cultural. The child is impelled to action not only by the standards of his society but by the total biological and psychological impact of the situation upon him. He cannot escape making his own choice according to such insight and foresight as he can muster.

When the child acts according to his own best choice, having been guided by such help as accepted standards can give, his action has the vigor, power, and "stick-to-itiveness" that we associate with strength of character and "will." The fact that the child has made his own choice allows the situation to act upon him with its full impact. He does not have to muster up "will," because the thing to be done is something that he *feels* as needing to be done. The driving power behind his action comes from the energies in the situation as well as from those in the child. It would take more "will" of the strictly subjective type, if such existed, to sidetrack his act than to complete it.

Yet his act is not an irresponsible movement along the line of least resistance. He uses his intelligence in making his choice. He can foresee, and be helped to foresee, the consequences of his act. His mental powers are the great contributions he can add to the enormous energies of his environment. His own energies and those of the environment complement one another in pushing his act forward toward completion. His personal effort consists largely of the hard thinking required to see his situation straight and clear. According to such insight as he has, he is caught up and carried along by the "will" of the situation.

Choice, Accountability, and the Creative Social Act

What makes the difference between a flabby and a sturdy, self-disciplined character? An understanding of the causes should help point the way to the cure.

One cause of weak character is too much living under conditions which place too little responsibility upon the individual. There are two components in responsibility—choice and accountability. The responsible person is one who is free to choose his own acts, and who is held accountable for the consequences of his choices. For example, in public life we fix responsibility by determining who the policy makers and the major decision makers are. We hold such persons accountable for the consequences of their policies and decisions.

Each person's responsibility in any common act is determined by the scope of the area in which he may exercise personal choice. Thus, if a laborer performs acts which result in the construction of a defective bridge, we do not hold him accountable if he is simply acting on decisions made by the designers and engineering staff. We hold the latter accountable, as being the responsible persons in this case. But within the framework of the decisions made by his superiors the workman has a degree of latitude in making his own decisions, and we hold him accountable within these limits.

The absence of either choice or accountability makes a farce of responsibility. For example, the characteristic features in the environment of what we commonly call the "spoiled" child are wide latitude for making choices combined with little accountability for consequences. When things go wrong, when unfortunate or unpleasant consequences are brought about by his own acts, he is in one way or another protected from suffering them. Some one else takes the brunt for him. If this becomes the pattern of his life, he develops an irresponsible attitude and character.

But the child's conduct becomes equally irresponsible if he lives in an environment characterized by a high degree of accountability with little or no opportunity for choice. If the child's major choices are made for him, he escapes the responsibility of having to make judgments where values and policies are at stake. The escape from the responsibility of making choices is what makes living under a dictatorship so charming for so many people, children, youths, and adults alike.

When teachers try to enlist student participation in cooperative problem-solving, it is a common experience to encounter resistance in students who have never done this before. Habituated to school life in which all major choices are made by adults and in which responsibility is limited to the successful following of directions and carrying out of orders, the child at first resents being pushed from this protected nest. He does not want to choose problems and plan attacks upon them. He asks the teacher to tell him what to do, and often considers the latter irresponsible or incompetent if he refuses to do so.

But once men and children experience responsibility and learn to accept it, they give it up only under coercion. Not only do they develop the courage to make choices and the hardiness to take the consequences, but they also acquire the conviction that the acceptance of responsibility is the road to freedom.

Efforts to build strength of character by emphasizing accountability while restricting choice are bound to fail because in point of fact there can be no accountability where there is no choice. The child does not feel personally accountable when he knows he is merely carrying out directions prescribed by others. If the results are not fruitful, he blames those who made his choices for him. This is the reason why such methods must rely for disciplinary effect upon rewards and punishments personally granted or imposed by teachers. The child cannot be made to feel accountable for the inherent consequences of acts he did not choose; hence consequences of another type must be invented and externally imposed. Such consequences discipline the child only as long as the teacher is on hand to impose them. Remove the teacher, with his invented consequences, and the child's "discipline" goes out the door, too. Sensing no personal accountability for the inherent consequences of his acts, the child behaves irresponsibly.

The distinction between inherent and externally imposed consequences must be made clear. It is one thing for a child to suffer the failure of his telegraph sounder to work because he did not study the principles of its operation before beginning work. It is quite another thing for him to suffer punishment imposed by a teacher who found him disobeying orders to build such an instrument. Similarly, it is one thing for him to enjoy the success of his instrument and quite another thing for him to enjoy the granting of a high grade for having carried out well some choice made for him by his teacher.

What makes a child flabby is not lack of externally imposed consequences. Rather it is protecting him from the inherent consequences of his own acts, assuming that he is permitted choice in the first place. In our desire to guarantee the success of children we may err twice: first by motivating him externally, and second by interfering in his activities when we see his ineptness and wish to forestall his experiencing failure. It is not easy to know when legitimate help and guidance are called for, and when we should not interfere in the natural course of events. But unless learning is seen as a process of experimental inquiry in which the experiments that fail may be as instructive as the experiments that succeed, we are liable to fail on the side of overprotection, with its softening effect upon character.

If executive quality is to be built into the character of children, they must have the opportunity to make choices and they must experience accountability for the consequences. The degree of responsibility to be placed upon them is a matter that must be determined by their maturity and their readiness. It will not help to expand the area of their free choice beyond the limits of their power to accept responsibility. This will only end in having to protect them from consequences that should never have been risked in the first place. But on the other hand, the area of choice should be stretched to the utmost of the children's powers. Just how far it can be stretched calls for the exercise of nice judgment on the part of those who guide the children, based on intimate knowledge of them, their lacks and their abilities.

But even more, a faith in the children is required—a faith in their ability to respond to challenges wisely made. It does not matter so much if errors are made in judging the degree of responsibility the children can assume, provided there exists a fundamental determination to broaden steadily the area of responsibility. Mistakes are inevitable and have the great merit of being the experiments on the basis of which a compensatory increase or decrease of the area of responsibility can be made. But the mistake of basing the whole direction of educational effort upon the continual shrinkage, rather than upon the continual expansion, of the area of responsibility is fatal.

One way to widen the area of personal choice is to recognize responsibility as a group function. Hierarchical arrangements in a group narrow the range of personal responsibility because each level in the hierarchy may make choices only within limits prescribed by policy set in the level above. While a few persons at the top of the hierarchy may appear to enjoy wide latitude in making choices, the majority at the bottom of the hierarchy operate within narrowly prescribed limits. Furthermore, lack of communication between the various levels makes the whole structure rigid, and in the end limits the choices of even those at the top of the hierarchy. Since policy cannot be set on the basis of free sharing of common experience, precedents harden into custom and prescribe all further action. The hierarchical head, while exercising a great deal of personal control over the individuals in the group, becomes as bound as they to the prescribed patterns of conduct.

But when responsibility becomes a group function, choices must be made and accountability assumed by the group. Every member personally shares in this. While basic choices are not made by him alone, he exercises personal responsibility in influencing them and in undergoing their consequences. This does not mean that the group may not delegate its responsibility to various members. In fact, no group can be effective without delegation of responsibility. In delegating responsibility to individual members, the group remains the ultimate authority. The group reviews the individual's actions, criticizes, endorses, repudiates. In contrast, a group's renunciation of responsibility makes it possible for one or more aggressive individuals to pretend to the authority the group fails to exercise. Instead of the individual being responsible to the group, he dominates the group, and his acts are no longer subject to review.

The child can find his strength of character within the creative social act. Participation in it gives him an opportunity to share in the making of choices and the assuming of accountability. The experience of many persons is brought to bear in making judgment wiser and hence action more effective. Conflicting values, with their paralyzing effect upon action, may be resolved through the mutual examination of experience. Goals may be brought into better relationship to the means of their attainment when the insights of many persons are applied to the task. A group is then able to make choices in which the combined efforts of its members harmonize with one another and with the natural resources and energies of the objective situation in which they find themselves. Each individual's strength is bolstered and supported by the fact that he is moving with and making use of the total complex of physical, social, and personal energies which define the situation. He leans upon and finds his strength in the executive quality of forces that transcend him.

The School Helps Rebuild the Social Order

As the school develops executive quality in the children, their activities penetrate progressively more deeply into the culture and exert a transforming influence upon it. The transformation is effected both by cultural diffusion and by social action.

By cultural diffusion is meant the intermingling in the culture of values and modes of life which originate at certain seminal concentrations of energies generated within the culture. There are centers where the energies of the culture interact to produce new forces that react reflexively upon the culture.

The school is capable of being such a center. When children in the creative social act reconstruct the habits and values they inherit from the culture, their new habits and values tend to diffuse back into and permeate the culture. This may occur in a number of ways.

For one matter the changing outlook and conduct of the children affect the families of which they are members. It is not uncommon for parents to oppose new patterns introduced by children. This is especially common in the conflict between the first and second generations of immigrant families. On the other hand there may not be any conscious sense of opposition, submission, and change. New modes may creep into and radically transform family life, yet scarcely be noticed.

The emerging values and habits of children may react upon the culture through their roles as consumers. Children as consumers influence our forms of entertainment and recreation, the content of newspapers and radio programs, even the designs of objects used primarily by adults. The demands and needs of children influence the purchase of television sets, the location of family housing, the planning of family finances. While many demands are common to all children, in every specific case these demands are colored by the values accepted by the children of that particular family.

Furthermore, changes in the life values of children often have a powerful delayed effect upon the culture. Values formed during school years help make the adult what he is and influence his impact on society.

Social action, in contrast to cultural diffusion, is the effort to transform some aspect of the culture through an organized assault planned and executed by a critical group. In recent decades America has witnessed an increasing number of instances of social action by groups of school children with their teachers, typified by such undertakings as the improvement of race relations in a given community, the improvement of community recreational facilities, or the increase of public sensitivity to some important social issue.[2]

Whether the transforming effect of the school upon society is the result of cultural diffusion or of social action, proposals that the school deliberately undertake to perform such a transforming function generally meet with opposition. If it is true that religious behavior has an executive quality in which present existence is transformed then such opposition must be regarded as a challenge to the proposal that the schools should seek to develop religious quality in the conduct of children.

The objection in America to effort by the school to transform the

[2] For examples see the Educational Policies Commission, *Learning the Ways of Democracy* (Washington, D. C.: National Education Association, 1940).

culture is not based merely on a leaning toward conservatism and traditionalism. It is based in part on a recognition of the fact that were any one point of view to capture the schools and to use them as a means of building its own strength by shaping the views of the children, then democracy in America would be threatened if not destroyed. This objection, however, makes an assumption which is open to question.

It is questionable that the only way to transform society through the schools is to turn the schools over to a special group which would transform society according to its blueprint. Such attempts are made constantly. They come from some of the most respected as well as suspect sources. There is need to increase, not decrease, alertness to the danger. But such attempts are not the only possible way of using the schools to transform society.

There is a difference between society transforming itself through its schools and society being transformed through the use of the schools by a special group. One way is democratic, the other authoritarian. The democratic way calls for the schools to be a public arena in which can meet a wealth of proposals coming from all quarters. It calls for criticism by the children and their teachers of both the existing culture and all ideas for modifying the culture. In contrast, the authoritarian way calls for the schools to be the mouthpieces of special ideological interests which claim exclusive right to be heard. Authoritarianism calls for the uncritical acceptance of either the existing culture or specified proposals for changing the culture. The Christian warning that no finite value judgment can be taken as final and correct reveals the irreligious character of the authoritarian way.

The Churchly and Sectarian Functions of the School

In some respects the school is in a position analogous to that of the church-type religious organization. As an institution representing all the people, the public school in America stands, like the church-type, above every social, economic, and political issue that confronts the nation. The school, as an institution, cannot take one side of an issue without placing itself in conflict with that part of society which takes the other side. Were it to do this, the school would no longer be the instrument of the entire community but the tool of whichever segment of society could capture and use it for its own ends. By standing above issues, the school in an acquiescent mood tolerates and respects the viewpoints of all groups whose children enter its doors. The school provides, or should provide, one of the great meeting grounds, where, despite the differences among them, all creeds, beliefs, and values meet to be examined in an atmosphere of mutual respect and justice.

But the church-type emphasizes only one side of religious experience; there is the other side emphasized by the sect. There should exist deviant groups and individuals who criticize the community, formulate their own ideals, and organize themselves for the purpose of realizing these ideals. If the school were to combine and integrate both the church function and the sect function, what might result is this: The school might serve its church function by bringing together children in an environment where the differences that divide society need no longer divide the children. The school might serve its sect function by respecting deviation, by encouraging deviant groups to develop themselves *without* loss of love and respect from the community, and by using deviation both as a means to inseminate society with new ideas and as a starting point from which to move toward unity.

Even though as a national institution the American school should stand above social issues, as a concrete local entity it should take positive stands on social issues. The executive mode in religious experience is not likely to be developed in schools that remain neutral on the burning issues of the day.

In what sense can the school both take a stand upon and yet remain above social issues? In the sense that stands should be arrived at through democratic processes, and that there should be simultaneous drives toward *both* unity and diversity.

Teachers and school administrators have not only a right but a responsibility to commit themselves to beliefs after the most careful and objective inquiry of which they are capable. It is to be expected, nevertheless, that the viewpoints of the teachers of America will show a range of diversity as great as that which is manifested in the culture itself. Similarly, children enter the classroom bringing with them a diversity of cultural outlooks and modes of behaving. The children and the teacher can use this diversity as starting points from which to work toward unity of outlook through the democratic sharing of experience. But participative attacks upon mutually recognized problems are likely, even as they create agreement in some areas, to create deviations in others. A cooperative attack upon a problem, even while arriving at mutually acceptable solutions, is likely at the same time to take the individual inquirers into new and diverse fields which stimulate in them new and diverse ideas.

Objectivity should not be confused with neutrality. It is to be expected of the teacher that he have values which he considers of sufficient worth to bring to the attention of children. To do less is to default as a teacher. Objectivity must be achieved not through neutrality but through the way in which inquiry is carried on in the classroom. The teacher's values and beliefs, like those of the children, are matters to be inquired into, not accepted without examination. They are to be inquired into by considering the relevant evidence, examining consequences, relating the claims in question to other accepted beliefs and values. Objectivity resides in the *methods* by which claims are investigated, *not* in maintaining neutrality.

Such methods should extend beyond the classroom to the relations of the teachers with one another, of school administrators with one another and with teachers, of school personnel with the lay members of the community.

Because such processes create diversity as well as unity, one would expect to find in the school the growth of a great variety of ideas challenging our traditional beliefs and loyalties. There should be no prejudging the worth of such views. The churchlike school, far from discouraging sectlike deviations in the culture, should insist that deviants be respected and given a hearing. It is for society to judge whether it desires to accept the contribution of a deviant group—but the difference between judging and prejudging must be kept clearly in mind.

Public education in America can perform both a churchly function in the movement toward unity and a sectarian function in the encouragement of diverse groups. By integrating the community, the school can help prevent the paralysis that results when the community is hopelessly shattered. By stimulating diversity the school can help ensure the fertilization society needs in order to keep moving ahead.

CHAPTER X

The Aesthetic Mode

The Dramatic and Consummatory Quality of Experience

THERE has always been a powerful aesthetic motif in religious experience. So far as we know, the fine arts originated in connection with the expression of religious feeling. Primitive man danced in order to express his feeling of communion with the spirit of the tribe. He made and wore masks so that he could dramatize the forces of good and evil into the vortex of whose conflict he felt swept. His sculpture symbolized and personalized the energies which sustained and threatened him in his life struggle. His painting and drawing, whether on the walls of his caves, of his skin shelters, or on his implements, portrayed and symbolized the resources upon which he was dependent and the dangers that made life precarious.

The conflict of good and evil is the persistent theme in the world's great art. The ancient Greek tragedies, the poetry of Dante, Goethe, and Milton, the music of Wagner, Beethoven, and Tchaikovsky, the dance of Martha Graham and Mary Wigman, express the dramatic poignancy of the situation in which man finds himself, caught up in the struggle of forces that transcend him. The art of social protest, such as the novels of Steinbeck, Hemingway, and Sinclair Lewis, the painting of Benton and Rivera, the plays *Tobacco Road* and *Dead End*, reflects man's resentment of the oppressiveness of evil. Such art in its bitterness implies stubborn determination to continue the struggle for the realization of human values and ideals.

Man finds life, nature, experience, and existence precarious, but he also finds that they have consummations which his efforts can sometimes help realize. This often leads to the idea that the universe is a vast fulfilment of conscious intent. God is eternal, complete, and finished because the complete and finished is aesthetically satisfying. The cosmologies of the great religions are aesthetically satisfying because they are closed and complete; their cosmogonies because they express the drama leading to the vast consummation represented in the completed cosmologies. Salvation, insofar as it is a consummation following the dramatic conflict of good and evil, is an aesthetic idea.

Art, like religion, is the effective organization of materials and energies, despite tensions and resistances, in such a way that there is movement to an inclusive and fulfilling consummation. Great art, like religion, expresses man's most inclusive aspirations and the drama involved in the struggle to realize them.

Our tendency to identify art with the fine arts has obscured the fact that art basically means the production of something desirable and worthwhile from materials whose very reluctance to be shaped to human ends calls out the skill and creativeness of the artisan or artist. The practical arts are the root form of all art. The farmer cultivating the soil, the mechanic adjusting the machine, the host putting his guests at ease, are all artists in the degree that they use materials and energies appropriately and imaginatively, and in the degree that their efforts end in satisfying consummation.

Most of the activities and pusuits of life are capable of being works of art. Making them so is the difference between brute existence and the cultivation of the divine. We have a choice—shall we be content with careless acts awkwardly performed or shall we seek to direct them appropriately toward consummations? When energies and materials are disorganized, when they are not adapted to their goal, when they clash with and cancel the effectiveness of one another—then we recognize both an act and a product which are ungainly and ugly. But when energies and materials are appropriately adapted to their ends, we have an act and a product that are beautiful. The economy of movement in the person who walks gracefully, the spontaneous ease of the person who manages his associations with others well, the creativity of a family that seeks to improve the quality of its living, each has its own beauty.

Art is more than the consummatory phase of experience. It includes the drama in the events that lead to consummation. One of the necessary conditions of art quality in experience is resistance to consummation. Were art identical with consummation, and did the organism move from disequilibrium to consummation without opposition, then the well-fed worm could be said to be having an aesthetic experience.

Resistance and the efforts of the individual to overcome resistance create a dramatic plot. Consummation is but one movement—the last—of the plot. When the outcome of movement toward consummation is in doubt, the individual experiences feelings of suspense, hope, despair. The earlier movements in the plot are an integral part of the complete artistic-aesthetic event. Without them consummation is flat and insipid. This is true both in the fine arts and in the practical art of living. Architecture and music without dynamic accent, drama without plot, life activity without resistance, are equally dull.

Art and Valuational Coherence

Dramatic plot and consummation—these are the two elements in which religion and art unite. Religion is the concern we feel as we watch the fate of our ideals in the struggle of existence. Religion is the ecstasy we feel in those moments when we are able to orient our view of self and universe so as to see coherence and harmony in the relation of the various forces at work.

Art, on its side, becomes great when its themes express the drama involved in the struggle for overarching values and ideals. Art that lacks a powerful idealistic motive tends to be merely pretty or brilliant instead of beautiful, or merely shoddy and ugly instead of tragic. A cinquain of Adelaide Crapsey may be a brilliant gem, but lacking the comprehensive value motivation to be found in such poetry as that of Whitman or Goethe, it cannot stand with the world's greatest poetry. Grant Wood's "Daughters of the American Revolution" may not be the greatest picture ever painted, but it has stature because it is not simply a picture of austere women but a savage protest against narrowness and bigotry. In contrast to most comic strips, political cartoons become art in proportion as they cut deeply into the core of human hopes and ideals. The Song of Solomon would be pornography were not its theme the realization of supreme blessedness. As one writer has pointed out, all great art is religious art; great "secular" art is simply art of an unrecognized religion.[1]

This is even more true of the art of living than of the fine arts. In their isolation and relative triviality the daily dramas and consummations of life may lack both artistic and religious quality. But place them in the setting of an evolving core of valuational coherence and their meaning increases. When we see life in relation to a considered and comprehensive end-in-view, we despair more, yet hope more; fear more, yet are more often transfixed with joy. Life's episodes become movements in an epic. At the same time, the inherently trivial and unimportant events of life are placed in their proper perspective and seen for what they are. We no longer make mountains out of molehills, but we do begin to see mountains where they actually exist.

To take a concrete example, note what happens to social efficiency when it is illuminated by a coherent multiplicity of ends rather than by isolated, narrow ends. Efficiency then changes from an unimaginative mechanization of activity to creative productivity. It becomes vitalized by an inspired idealism. For example, a housing development involving the construction of several thousand homes becomes ugly and depressing if it is motivated only by the desire to provide shelter on an economical mass-production basis. The uni-

[1] L. Buermyer, *The Esthetic Experience*, p. 150.

formity of the rows of streets and houses makes such a community drab enough, and the lack of adequate provision for such essentials of community life as shopping and recreation turns such a development into a barren desert. In the name of efficiency the planners and builders of such a place do only a routine job and deprive not only themselves but others of creative experience.

The story is different when economy is retained as an end but integrated with a variety of other ends having to do with building a community with resources for good living. Ingenuity goes into the work of planning how to vary the designs and landscaping or the houses in interesting and beautiful ways, while still keeping such variety compatible with the demands and economies of mass production. Streets are laid out to make economical use of the land while still providing for shopping, recreation, education, and the cultivation of a variety of community interests. That the aim is to accomplish all this while still retaining the benefits of new methods of large-scale construction makes the undertaking all the more challenging. The integration of multiple values challenges the faith, vision, courage, and creativity of the participants in the enterprise. It encourages them to develop the qualities associated with artistic and religious personalities.

Mystical Experience

When the art of living becomes great, it is likely to acquire a degree of mystical quality. In living greatly a man integrates conflicting values and sees life whole. The opposition between the ego and the world tends to disappear. The individual subdues neither the world nor the self; rather he learns to orient himself in relation to the world in such a way that energies reinforce instead of cancel one another.

Mystical experience is probably at once the most intense religious and aesthetic experience known to man. The descriptions of mystical experiences given us by those who have them[2] have this in

[2] A number of these have been brought together by William James, *The Varieties of Religious Experience*.

common: that the experience culminates in an ecstatic sense of union with nature, God, or the universe, and that this comes only as the result of a prolonged struggle to reorganize the self in harmony with the universe of value and reality. Men whose major life activities habituate them to seeking a synthesis of many claims are the ones most likely to have mystical experiences. Not only the religious mystics, but poets, philosophers, mathematical physicists, and the leaders of idealistic social experiments are likely to have a strain of mysticism in their make-up.

Nevertheless, mystical experiences are had in some degree by almost everyone. To identify the meaning of mystical experience with supernaturalism obscures its meaning, for the experience is often had by naturalistically inclined and religiously skeptical persons. Its simplest, most everyday forms are the sympathy and empathy experienced among members of a closely knit social group, such as a family or circle of intimate friends who share a community of experience and understanding. Another example, experienced by most persons, is the response to mountain, forest, and sky with a sense of harmony and unity.

The sense of union with the environment depends upon the degree to which the forces in the environment and one's self seem to reinforce one another. When they do, the barriers that mark off an individual's separate existence dissolve. The self expands to include a wider community—the whole universe when mystical experience is at its height. The world is no longer alien, filled with obstacles and threats to life. Instead the world and the self are confluent with one another and together form a new self.

The ease with which such a feeling comes upon one who is communing with field, stream, and forest suggests that on such occasions symypathetic responses resultant from the primordial relationship of organism and environment are stirred into being. But when this relationship is complicated by the multifarious arrangements of complex social life, the sense of union is not so easily achieved. The individual is caught in conflicting pressures and claims. Yet he still seeks coherence and harmony.

Mystical experience is the consummation of consummations, in that it is the result of the integration of all partial values. The little consummations of a limited living and experiencing join together in one immense consummation when the individual is able so to reorganize his relationship to the natural and social universe that all values and the means to their attainment come together in a harmonious whole. That few attain such a state of bliss, and that no man can or would even want to remain permanently in such a state, is attested to by the mystics themselves. Yet the working ideal of the maximum integration of life forces and values can be accepted by everyone.

Art and Community

Art in the most profound sense is the deliberate cultivation of all human activities to improve their quality. Every society produces a culture. A culture is the coherent yet richly variegated product of the society's cultivation of its many activities. The primary business of any society is to produce a culture of such variety, richness, and quality that all its members may find therein the means of their self-fulfilment. To be humane, society must cultivate the arts of living and produce therefrom a civilization that is aesthetically satisfying to all its members.

When men freely share with one another the arts they have cultivated, they improve the quality of the life lived by all. Arts are transmissive from person to person and from group to group. The process of acculturation is a process of enriching a culture through the mutual sharing of arts. Any culture is impoverished when barriers among groups interfere with acculturation.

Any well-developed art, whether practical or fine, is a cultivation and refinement of some aspect of experience. Hence acculturation in effect is a free sharing of experience. The artist does not necessarily intend to communicate anything. His concern is to produce from his materials the most inclusively satisfying object possible. But his creative acts produce many-valued consummations. Though communication may not have been intended, such acts do communicate to others the possibility of experiencing the same consummations. Art is a form of communication because it expresses from experience a maximum of meaning which may be shared with others.

Art makes possible the universally shared life. Whenever men learn to share without reservation all their arts with one another, we shall experience both the universal community and a life of such completely aesthetic quality as the world has never known.

CHAPTER XI

The Aesthetic Mode: Education

THE NEED FOR AESTHETIC QUALITY IN EDUCATION

THE aesthetic poverty of our schools would appall us were it not for the fact that habituation to it has dulled our sensitivities. Many of our children are sent to live a major part of their day in a dreary room whose walls are lined with funereal blackboards and whose ugly furniture is arranged in rows with deadening uniformity. The glaring, uncurtained windows have no live green thing growing on their ledges. The bareness of the walls, painted some nondescript color, is only accentuated by the occasional picture of George Washington that hangs in the same place year after year.

The drabness of the physical surroundings would perhaps be bearable were it not for the even greater drabness of the activities that are commonly carried on in such rooms. The drone of lessons being recited, the painful pauses while children grope for answers to the endless barrage of questions, the cumulative boredom of hour after hour and day after day of the same routine, contribute to a barren existence. It is no wonder that with the sounding of the bell both the teachers and the children rush to escape into the out-of-school world where life is not so perseveringly and systematically stripped of its variety and color.

The life of the school is often a life without disturbances, plot, and consummations. This is why the school seems so unreal and artificial to many. It is when one is face to face with beauty that, encountering the full quality of events, he experiences reality.

The unaesthetic nature of the school is in itself sufficiently deplorable. But the seriousness of the problem is intensified when the realization comes home that not merely the aesthetic life but the very spiritual life of the child is stunted in such an environment.

It is too much for the imagination to believe that life lacking in drama, color, and challenge can help a child develop a burning set of working ideals and a disposition to pursue them with joy and eagerness. The dullness of such a life does not increase his faith in the transformability of existence for the better. The lack of opportunity to join with others in the experiencing of beauty and to share with one another the culminations and consummations of activities carried out together does not build a glowing sense of community. The ennui into which the individual in a debilitating environment falls does not encourage in him the aggressive spirit that a militant faith calls for, nor even the attitude of deep contemplation that exists when religion is in an acquiescent mood.

In order to become aesthetically satisfying and thereby promote the religious life of the children, the school must help children have experiences of the kind which mobilize their energies and culminate in deeply satisfying outcomes. The children need to be confronted by the kinds of problems that challenge their eagerness, resourcefulness, and creativity. There need to be problems which, being genuinely felt as such by the child, have an element of precariousness. It is to be granted that many of the problems of this type will be only partially solvable by the children; some not at all. But the element of doubt, the feeling of exploring uncharted ground, the knowledge that both success and failure are possible, challenge enthusiastic response and create the plot interest which is the necessary prelude to the flood of feeling that characterizes aesthetic consummation.

One does not forget the absorption and suspense displayed by a group of children who have a set of white rats on experimental diets and do not yet know the outcome; who are trying to culture protozoa and are waiting for the day when they can first find them under their microscopes; who are writing a play and are anxious to see how the audience receives it the day it is presented; who are conducting a community campaign for better race relations and are half-fearful, half-hopeful about the community response; who are building a classroom grocery store and are anticipating the day when they can first put it into operation; who are constructing working models of time-telling devices used throughout history and have yet to see them operate. The culminations of such activities, when they are successful, are events to be celebrated and remembered. The fact that the remembrance of such events by the children does actually elicit in them a spirit of commemoration and celebration is proof enough of the aesthetic quality that enters into such experiences.

Helping the Child Experience the Qualitative Richness of Reality

To have an aesthetic experience a child must be wholly involved both in the consummation and the dramatic events that precede consummation. It is not enough that he be intellectually involved; he must be emotionally involved as well. The tendency of the school to treat every experience as though it were an intellectual affair alone accounts for much of the drabness and lack of imaginative quality in school life.

The following is an account of a study of evolution made by a group of seventh-graders. The imaginative, almost poetic, approach made to the study is in contrast to the coldly intellectual approach sometimes made to this same topic.

The children painted a colorful mural around three walls of their classroom which depicted such scenes as the creation of the earth according to the nebular hypothesis, the physical changes on the earth following its creation, the development of the first primordial protoplasm, the parade of plant and animal life evolving therefrom up to and including man.

The children played many recorded musical selections and used their powers of discrimination and imagination in order to select those pieces which for them expressed the mood suggested by each phase of the story of evolution as they had painted it. (For example, Debussy's

La Mer was selected for the mood of suspenseful quiet suggested by the scene of the cooled and waiting earth shortly before the appearance of the first life. "The Storm" from the *William Tell* overture expressed the violence of the scene depicting the earth's split from the sun.) The children wrote verses in which they sought to express the mood of each scene.

The culminating activity was the presentation of a finished performance to another group of children invited to the classroom—a performance in which the murals and the poetry read to the background of the music were used to re-create the drama of the whole majestic story. When the performance ended with the triumphant music of Tchaikovsky's Fourth Symphony and with the verses expressing the emergence of man and his spiritual aspirations, there was without doubt a consummatory experience which was both aesthetic and religious.

Not only was the above experience dramatic and consummatory, but also it brought the children closer to reality than a merely intellectual approach to the problem could have done. The difference between the intellectual and the aesthetic approach to reality is the difference between a series of abstract or descriptive statements about reality and the direct experience of reality.

Had the intellectual approach been relied upon exclusively in the example given, the children would have studied the abstract laws involved in the theory of evolution, or the concrete description, as established by science, of the various developments in the history of evolution. Whether abstract or concrete and descriptive, the material would simply have pointed to and told about something not experienced by the children. Instead, the aesthetic approach to the topic brought it to life for them. In effect they lived through the history of evolution. They did more than study some abstract laws *about* reality and some concrete descriptions *of* reality; the drama and consummation they experienced *were* reality.

The intellectual and the aesthetic approaches need not and should not be mutually exclusive. The aesthetic approach taken alone would likely degenerate into a fanciful flight to a made-up dream world. Without a firm grounding in scientific fact and theory, the children's imaginative re-creation of the events of evolution would have been no more than a figment of their imaginations. Their imaginations were able to bring them face to face with reality because they based everything they did upon solid research into the laws and facts involved.

In the degree that their research was defective, they failed by that much to encounter reality. For example, in the illustration cited some persons might criticize them and their teacher for having uncritically accepted the nebular hypothesis of the earth's origin, since there is evidence to support other hypotheses. But no matter how valid their scientific background became, the reality of what they were studying could not come to life until they moved beyond "statements about" and "descriptions of" to the actual aesthetic experience which alone brings one into direct contact with the immediate qualitativeness of things.

The following illustration shows how this interplay of scientific description and artistic creativity brought one child closer to reality than he could have come in the absence of either factor:

> The seventh-year group hatched some chicken eggs in a small incubator which had been made by a committee of children using a wooden crate, some insulating board, an electric lamp for heat, and an inexpensive thermostat. During the tweny-one days of waiting for the chicks to hatch, the children studied about the development of the chick embryo from books and pictures. They even opened one egg each day in order to discover at firsthand each new development. But it was during the playing of Moussorgsky's "Ballad of the Unhatched Chick" from *Pictures at an Exhibition* that one child cried in delight, "I could just *see* that chick inside his shell!"

The fact that both scientific and aesthetic subject matter happen to be involved in the above example should not be permitted to obscure the significance of what it illustrates. Not the subject matter but the quality of the experience is what we are interested in. Any study carried on by children, whether primarily historical, aesthetic, or anything else, has scientific quality as long as the children are attending carefully to the need to establish, verify, and interpret facts. Any study, regardless of the subject matter, and even in the complete absence of artistic or aesthetic materials, has aesthetic quality as long as the children and teacher are managing their joint enterprise in such a way that it has dramatic and consummatory quality. Contrariwise, studies involving scientific subject matter can be handled in ways that are entirely unscientific in quality, and studies involving artistic or aesthetic subject matter can be handled in ways entirely lacking in dramatic and consummatory quality. Not the subject matter but the manner and method of handling it determine the quality of an activity.

It is essential to the religious development of the child that scientific and aesthetic quality mutually support one another in all his experiences to bring him into direct and full contact with reality. Unless he actually feels the things he studies about—unless he experiences them aesthetically as well as grasps them intellectually—he will leave school and enter his life occupations with a feeling that he is escaping from a world of unreality into the world of reality. Too many persons have left school with just this feeling, and it is for this reason that the ideals the schools have sought to instill in the consciousness of the child have so often been in vain. If we want the child to develop faith in the transformability of existence, we had better help him keep in contact with the very stuff that has to be transformed.

The aesthetic mode should pervade the entire life of the school and should be a criterion of its educational adequacy. Unless the child experiences consummations cumulatively and continuously, he cannot maintain his implicit faith in the potential improvability of life. And yet, unless he experiences the challenge and the struggle that precede consummation, he cannot develop the moral fiber needed to keep pushing toward a better life. In his aesthetic experiences he touches the qualitative reality of existence. He comes as close as he ever will to that communal relation with existence which at once sustains him yet inspires him to renewed effort. By experiencing the qualitative richness of reality, the child has an opportunity to select and integrate the values which become the ideals motivating his life.

CHAPTER XII

The Contemplative Mode

The Importance of Cultic Symbolism

In the contemplative mode a group or community celebrates and commemorates the values with which it identifies itself, for the purpose of renewing the group's strength and mobilizing its energies for action. This is a mode which, in the orthodox religions, is associated with prayer, worship, and ritual.

Yet it is a mode which appears in the common life of all men, whether they recognize it as a religious mode or not. Every well-knit family, every clique of intimate friends, most age, sex, occupation, and class groups, have innumerable rituals and signs, many of them informal and not consciously recognized, by which the members remind themselves of their belonging to one another and of the values by which the group lives. A father's homecoming whistle, a bobby-soxer's characteristic costume, the type of home furnishings characteristic of members of the middle class, have conscious and unconscious meanings for the persons involved which go far beyond the nominal functions they serve of announcing an arrival, protecting the body, or making a house livable. They are symbols which evoke in the participants a wide range of feelings and emotions. They somehow sum up and express the meanings accrued in countless past experiences with one's own group—meanings that are nonrational and cannot be expressed in logical discourse.

Every group—the individual family unit, American hobodom, the members of a given trade or profession, a nation—tends consciously or unconsciously to develop its own ritualistic symbolism composed of special mannerisms, vocabulary, places of meeting, and innumerable other things. Almost any event or object in the group's life, whether incidental to or central in its activities, is capable of being elevated to a place of importance in the group's consciousness as symbolic of what the group feels in its common memories and hopes. By such symbolism the group expresses consciousness of itself and its aspirations.

Among established religious groups myth, ritual, liturgy, sacrament, standardized forms of worship and prayer, and such items as the crucifix, the steeple, the ringing of bells, the sounding of gongs, certain habits of dress and articles of clothing, are among the standard cultic symbols. It is possible more or less consciously to plan and choose a system of cultic symbolism to express meanings deemed most worthy by the group. This is why the ritualism of the common life can become refined into the liturgy of an established religion.

But while rituals and symbols may themselves be consciously chosen, the meanings they express can never be made fully explicit. Though these meanings evolve from common activities and occupations, and hence should be as testable in experience as any other meanings, they cut too deeply into the whole of life, with the latter's inseparable combining of reason and emotion, consciousness and unconsciousness, rationality and irrationality, to be expressible without the aid of the rich resources of music, poetry, and art.

The power of cultic symbolism to arouse and mobilize for action the full energies of an individual and of a group is enormous. Such symbolism can tap the deepest wellsprings of action and evoke conduct of undreamed vitality and power. It reaches and touches the nonrational energies which reason alone cannot penetrate.

Authoritarian states and churches recognize this and often turn the power of cultic symbolism to their own ends. The result is a corruption which impels free people to turn away in disgust. Distrust and fear of cultic symbolism have characterized modern democratic-scientific culture. Cultic practices have been used both to stifle democracy and to oppose science and reason. Infamous men and institutions have cleverly misused cultic symbolism to further their own narrow ends. We have learned to associate cultic symbolism with superstition, ignorance, blind emotionalism, and authoritarianism.

The reasons for our distrust go even deeper than this, however. We have come to distrust emotion itself and to place our faith solely in rationality as the means of improving the quality of existence. One of the strongest trends running through the history of Western civilization is its tendency to identify emotion with man's brute nature and reason with his divine nature.

Among the Greeks, intellectual activity acquired enormous prestige because it was primarily an occupation of the free citizen, whose leisure was made possible by the slave economy. Manual labor took on the degradation of the social class which performed it. In Greek society, man sentenced the human body to the kind of labor brutes could perform and reserved for the human mind the activities that were associated with excellence and refinement. Since the emotions were thought to be physical, they shared in the body's inferiority. For Plato the good life consisted of the release of the mind from the corporeal ties which chained it to earth, so that it could soar into the realm of disembodied Truth and Beauty and contemplate their pure forms forever.

The exaltation of mind and degradation of body received a fresh impetus when Platonism and Christianity joined forces in later centuries. The Christian tendency to identify sin with the body and its emotions reduced the body from mere brutishness to sheer nastiness. At the same time the Greek identification of mind with man's soul, understood as his essential or distinguishing trait, became associated with the religious idea of the soul as the essence of man's divinity.

Then, on top of all this, came modern science with its intention and aspiration of rationalizing the whole of existence. The result of this confluence of forces is that Western man tends to exalt the qualities associated with mind and rationality, and to distrust deeply those qualities associated with the body, the emotions, and nonrationality. Even the Catholic faith, for all its pageantry and color, is a less aesthetic and more intellectual religion than any of the great Oriental religions. And even the ritualism of Catholicism was too much for Protestantism, which stripped itself as bare of aesthetic accessories and tone as it could.

But democratic people need to learn that there is nothing inherently evil in cultic symbolism—that it is a power that can and should serve the ends of democratic living. When cultic symbolism is left in authoritarian hands, it is inevitably put to authoritarian use. But there is no reason why each group, from the smallest and most intimate, such as the family, to the greatest, such as the international community, cannot develop its own symbolism democratically through the contributions of all members. Cultic practices should evolve from the common life of the group, changing and growing with the reconstruction of the body of integrated value to which the group commits itself.

Reason and emotion need no longer be seen as mutually exclusive and antagonistic. Though cultic symbolism expresses the rationally inexpressible, it is capable of examination and revision to make it coherent with reality. The emotions worth having are those that integrate with one's scientific view of the world. Emotions based on rational insight and understanding are the deepest and most powerful of all feelings because they are backed and reinforced by intellect.

We cannot escape the cult, anyway. Even science, the epitome of rationality, becomes a cult shot through with its own symbolism. The test tube expresses for the scientist his loyalty to the authority of experimental method rather than to the authority of persons. It should not be otherwise, for this demonstrates that the cult, far from being the tool of ignorance and authoritarianism, can be used to intensify our loyalty to the things that fight ignorance and authoritarianism.

While intellect is indispensable, pointing as it does to reality, the aesthetic response to the world actually touches reality. In reality we find our values and ideals. Recognizing this, we should accept cultic symbolism as an indispensable aid in holding close to ourselves the ideals we cherish.

Myth as Illustrative of Cultic Symbolism

The myth is a cultic type which serves to illustrate cultic function. Like all cultic symbolism, myths express truths not statable in logical discourse. This idea contrasts with two less critical attitudes toward myths—that they are literally true, and that they are nonsense to be explained away by reference to the psychosocial needs which led men to create them. A critical approach to myth seeks to understand what it metaphorically expresses.

The nature and function of myth have perhaps never been described better than by Preston T. Roberts, in the following words:

> Mythology, in the widest and most general sense, is that living body of uncriticized and fundamental notions, that largely unconscious yet undergirding theory of interpretation, or that broadly imaginative ordering or giving shape to experience that arouses the activity, elicits the feeling, and crystallizes the meaning of a people's collective existence. Mythology of this order operates at levels far deeper and richer than the mind, and exercises an urgency of control more compelling than the intellect can ever command. It provides and defines the vision of the world and of man with which they see.
>
> In a stricter sense, mythology refers to that concrete body of stories and legends preserved in the popular memory which is the unconscious creation and inheritance of the common life. Myths in this sense are a recording, a distillation, and a celebration of the facts of ordinary human experience. Myths of this kind are the fragmentary fossil remains of the grass roots of human thought and feeling, the most sensitive index to the story of human striving that we have. They are the prod-

ucts of that marvelously assimilative faculty a people possesses whereby they can transform ordinary events into symbols far more concretely allusive and imaginatively real than the wooden abstractions of propositional statement can ever be. They keep alive the hidden strivings of the human spirit by giving them telling shape, deliver men from the narrow bounds of private worlds to endow their lives with a wider meaning and a deeper sanctity, express the elemental traits of human character and constantly, beneath varying guises, capture the primitive cyclic patterns of birth, death and renewal, and enable a people to reenact their past and reaffirm their common lot and destiny. Myths of this character release the magnificent and unsuspected energies for expression and action lying far behind and beyond the small circle of man's educated consciousness. They are the preconscious means whereby the vast and obscure reaches of common humanity participate imaginatively and concretely in realities far more complex and important than they ever know.

An example of a myth with this curiously specialized character is the body of stories and folklore and song which have clustered around and cast a glow of significance about the simple, obscure figure of John Henry. No one knows for sure where John Henry was born. All we know is that he died while building a tunnel for a railroad shortly after the Civil War. The songs that have grown up around him are work songs, wrung from the simple but compellingly concrete rhythms of heavy toil, rhythms responsive to the rise and fall of the hammer. The pattern of the verses is unmistakable, though not consciously designed by its many makers. John Henry, backed by his white boss in a contest against the new steam drill, won the bet but died from the strain. The story provided a plastic symbol for many things. Many a man, in singing its simple refrains, has been enabled to participate in processes and realities more rich and full in scope than the symbols taken literally by themselves apprehend. For the myth of John Henry dramatized and made accessible to the human heart the dark tragedy of the black man subjected to the power of the white; the inexorable fate of the worker in the early, desperate stages of industrialism, when he blindly felt that survival depended on matching his strength with that of the encroaching machine; the violent gutting of nature, which ruthless exploitation of the West could bring; the mingled glory and horror in existence, whereby all good is inextricably mixed with evil and whereby the arc of man's rise to his ripest, most full and heroic stature, is a broken arc, ending in death. For the rhythms and meanings of the John Henry refrains are those of an exultant chant, undercut by a deep strain of haunted sadness. They strike at the heart of human existence, catch elemental patterns of recurrence, evoke the typical and the universal, root life in its communal basis, join men together in an imaginative order, invest the hard realities of daily life with a ceremonial dignity, and convey an enlarged sense of the way what happened to John Henry once upon a time can happen to any man at any time.

The value of myth for a people therefore is this: its unexcelled expression and celebration of community, wherein all achievement is a collaboration and where a thousand think and feel as one.[1]

The reality of which myth talks is a dramatic world of action and resistance in which man is involved. Here all objects are friendly or threatening, familiar or mysterious, alluring or repelling. Such objects are in contrast to the objects of science, which are abstracted from the reality of the essentially aesthetic and axiological world that men experience daily. Science reduces colors to numbers stating wave frequencies—numbers which are useful in understanding and controlling reality, but which are a poor substitute for reality itself. It would be an inadequate discourse which found number more real than color. Scientific discourse can point to the logical aspects of reality, but values are experienced in reality which can only be expressed, if not in the metaphor of myth, then in some other symbolic form.

The mythos of modern Western democracy includes a great body of story and legend built around the concepts of freedom and equality. The Abraham Lincoln log-cabin legend, the sagas connected with the Westward movement, our pioneer songs, the Paul Bunyan stories, the folklore dealing with the customs and mores of capitalism, are part of a great culture myth expressive of what is called "The American Dream."

Freedom and equality share the characteristics of all other mythical beliefs. The American believes in their actual existence, and his faith in their reality cannot be shaken by any amount of pointing at the obvious inequities and restrictions of American

[1] From an unpublished paper. Quoted by H. N. Wieman, *The Source of Human Good*, pp. 144-146. Copyright 1945 by The University of Chicago Press. Reprinted by permission.

life. He is right—not perfectly right, but right. Freedom and equality do exist as realities in many aspects of American life, where they are experienced every day by many persons. Faith in them becomes unshakable because they are believed realizable as ideals. The discouraging thing about the American faith is that it so often seems not only unshakable but also blind. There is need not only to believe in freedom and equality as ideals, but to be more aware of the steps that must be taken to realize them.

The trouble with the folklore of democracy is not that it exists and is believed in, but that it is believed so uncritically. Our American legends could be beautifully expressive of our ideals if they were accompanied by critical consideration of what must be done to transform the ideals into reality. Such criticism would tend to rebuild the meanings of the stories themselves. We need a new generation of myth builders.

CHAPTER XIII

The Contemplative Mode: Education

The Spontaneous Growth of Cultic Symbolism

CULTIC practices have in the past been no stranger in the school. They have on the whole tended to symbolize authoritarian rather than democratic values. For many children the teacher is the stern symbol of the school's power to order his life. The very scene of the child's working day, the schoolroom with its straight rows of desks, is the symbol of the conformity and docility expected.

The school has not failed to reinforce such symbolism with appropriate ritualism. In ordinary life one speaks to his associates freely and naturally, but in school one observes the rituals of hand-raising, standing beside one's desk, and coming before the class even to make a simple comment. Teachers upon entering the classroom often leave everything that is spontaneous, warm, and human in their personalities outside and shroud themselves in the ritualistic robes of formality and ceremony. Whether deliberately or unconsciously, they manage to make the gradebook and the catechizing question the symbols of their authority.

The trouble is not the existence of ritualism in the schools, but rather that the values symbolized are the wrong ones arrived at by the wrong processes. There are schools, too few in number, in which the forming of a circle of chairs replaces the raised hand as the rite accompanying conversation; where the friendly pat on the shoulder instead of the command of the drill sergeant expresses the prevalent quality of human relations; where the question becomes a symbol of honest doubt and curiosity instead of a weapon; and where "How do you know?" and "Why?" appearing on the lips of students and teachers alike have almost a sacred quality expressing the fact that authority rests in experience and in facts rather than in persons.

The cultus too prevalent in the schools is repulsive because it is a synthetic manufactured by adults in order to persuade children uncritically to accept adult values and standards. In contrast, when the creative social act becomes both the end and the method of education, the cultus grows out of the common life and shared experiences of the children. Under such conditions both the teachers and the children adopt unconscious rituals which promote the common life. A dependable let's-talk-it-over attitude in the face of disagreements or ruffled feelings promotes a style of group living in which the pulling forward of a chair becomes recognizable to everyone as the signal for composing oneself and preparing to look at objective facts. Children encouraged month after month to participate in group planning develop their own rituals of writing down questions and subquestions, names and assigned tasks, on blackboards where all may see. Habituated to challenging the authority on which statements are made by one another, children often adopt a ritual of quizzing which they expect to be observed almost ceremoniously on such occasions as the completion of a progress report by one group to another.

Are these really rituals, or are they not after all simply conditioned responses? Doubtless they are both, but their ritualistic quality is shown by the way that the children depend upon them as signs that the democratic values they are learning to cherish are actually operating. Such acts are reminders, reassurances about accepted ways of doing things.

As children share experiences which are aesthetically satisfying, they build a set of common memories whose recall can renew the child's awareness of the values previously experienced. The experience of joining with others in the calling up of old memories is perhaps even more richly satisfying than the original experience itself.

There is deep enjoyment in reminding one another of the time that the group so successfully organized a school weather bureau, investigated a critical community problem, put on a play. The recall of intimate details—the particulars of what this or that person did, the humorous side lights, the difficulties and how they were met—gives the whole experience a warm glow. A feeling of comradeship envelops the group. Looking back gives a new perspective to and mellows the original experience. Without it being said, a sense of the significance of what was done hangs over the group. Without consciously meaning to, the group is celebrating both the values found most dear in previous experience and the values of present community.

Although the following is taken from family rather than school life, it illustrates the concept being discussed.

When Kay S. was three years old, her father held her on his lap and read to her on Christmas Eve Clement Moore's well known poem, "The Night Before Christmas." Each Christmas Eve thereafter this has been repeated. When Kay was five years old, her sister Jane was born, and during the succeeding years the reading of this poem on Christmas Eve became more and more a ceremonial event. As the two daughters became older, they would sit on either side of their father on the family sofa, and mother and other relatives would be present. After the reading, refreshments came to be served, and talk would follow about Christmas celebrations of former years. As time went on, the ceremony became more and more elaborate. Candles were lit while other lights were extinguished; the conversational aftermath lengthened. Nothing ever deterred Kay and Jane from being at home on Christmas Eve; dates with boys, even after their engagments had been announced, were not made; once Kay did not accept an invitation to a much desired trip so that she might be at home for "the reading." After Kay's marriage, she and her husband came to her parents' home on Christmas Eve in order to be present for the event. This practice has been continued down to the present time, both by Kay and her husband and by Jane and her husband. Last year, "father" read to both daughters, their husbands, three grandchildren and grandmother.[1]

The factorylike atmosphere of the school, with its demand that we move "efficiently" and quickly from task to task, makes us insensitive to the need for and the value of such experiences as the above. We feel such a compulsion to get the required tasks done that too seldom do we have the leisure to savor and enjoy the value of what is being done. Of course, if there is little satisfaction in the work to start with, there can be little point in taking time to recall and dwell happily upon it. But assuming the original aesthetic quality of experiences, there are compelling reasons why children should have the opportunity to refresh their memory of them.

The celebration of values formerly experienced prevents them from dying in consciousness. But not only are values vivified; in the process they are purified by being integrated with one another. The children are looking back at them from the perspective gained by the living they have done since. Things once important seem less so now; may even be laughed at goodnaturedly and tolerantly. And what once seemed a minor value may now be seen as the really significant part of what happened. Experience has a natural integrity and continuity; present experience illuminates the old experience in such a way as to change the latter's meaning and significance. And, turnabout, the recall of old values illuminates what is now happening to the child. He may leave one of the friendly sessions of recalling old memories with a new perspective on some of the projects he now has underway.

The ritualistic nature of these commemorative experiences is shown by the part that symbolism plays in them. The group

[1] Reprinted by permission from "Ritual in Family Living," by James H. S. Bossard and Eleanor S. Boll, *American Sociological Review*, p. 464, August, 1949. Bossard and Boll have recently published a study of family ritual based on data from almost four hundred families. See their *Ritual in Family Living* (Philadelphia: University of Pennsylvania Press, 1950).

seizes upon some item in its memories to symbolize the particular value which it loves to keep fresh in consciousness. Some trivial act of one of the members, some article made by someone, even a word or phrase that was used with some special significance in the remembered experience—almost anything is capable of becoming associated in memory with some fundamental value. A mere reference to the item can at almost any time remind the whole group of what it shares and holds dear.

Thus a system of cultic symbolism spontaneously and often unconsciously emerges in the shared activities of a group working together cooperatively and creatively. An understanding and sensitive teacher can encourage this by being aware of what is happening and by entering freely into the process to help the children identify and cultivate the things worth remembering. If he has the relation of camaraderie with the students which is both necessary to and grows out of joint participation in the creative social act, the cultic gestures that so spontaneously become a part of the children's behavior become a part of his behavior, too. Both his leadership in this and his falling in with the children when they take the lead help insure the appropriateness of what is done and give the children the support, not merely of adult sanction, but of adult participation.

The Elaboration of Cultic Symbolism

Were the foregoing as far as the cultic life of a group developed, it would perhaps be enough. But further refinements of great value may be undertaken. It is possible to help a group explicitly define the values it is experiencing. Did a project turn out better because Jerry learned to share better with others? Did the fish in the aquarium thrive because experimentation showed better ways of caring for them? Did drawing upon the riches of the cultural heritage throw further meaning upon some social problem being studied? Looking back upon experiences to define the exact nature of their qualitative goodness can be among the most educative of experiences. The values of cooperating, of using experimental methods of inquiry, of evaluating authority, are learned by practicing and experiencing them; but, once they are experienced, looking back upon them makes it possible to analyze and understand them. They then stand out in sharp definition and are heightened in consciousness. As ideals they lose their vagueness and become principles which can be described in terms of actual operations to be performed.

Once values are thus made sharp and explicit, they can be deliberately and creatively celebrated. On occasions set aside especially for the purpose the group can plan appropriate ceremonies.

These ceremonies, to be worth-while, would have to be different from the stereotyped, wooden gestures children are often required to perform at commencements, installations of class officers, flag ceremonies, and other occasions. The ceremony from first to last should be the children's own creation, growing out of their own experiences and expressing their own feelings.

The traditional media and materials can be used—pageantry, color, music, the burning of candles, choral speaking. But the movements in the ceremony should be worked out and planned by the children. The words and lines should be their own, written to express the meanings they have experienced and known. Or lines can be selected by the children from the writings of great artists because they express exactly something the children feel but may not be quite able to say. Selection, if done in this spirit, can be as creative as original writing—the artist used by the children is simply in harmony with them and makes a contribution to a creative process already going on in them, even though his work may have been done years before. Preferably the music used by the children should also be their own production, but unfortunately the poverty of our schools has made music so strange and distorted an experience for most children that compromise at some point less than ideal will usually have to be made. But basically the celebration can be the children's own creation, expressing not what they have been asked to feel or told they ought to feel, but what they actually do feel.

Why is it that the sensitive observer leaves so many school ceremonies with a feeling of disgust and revulsion? Part of the reason is that he senses the basic immorality of asking children to celebrate sentiments which they neither feel nor understand. We dedicate our schools to freedom; then fetter the child's mind with ideas he has no chance to examine and criticize. Do we have a gnawing suspicion that some of these ideas could not stand examination and criticism? We should, because probably they cannot. Consider the typical commencement, for example. The caps and gowns. The valedictorian. The innumerable prizes for accomplishment, especially for scholarship. What is being celebrated here? The virtues of competitive superiority, or the virtues of shared experience? The authority of a mortarboard or the authority of plain, undecorated competence? There was a time when these obscenities were committed only in the colleges, but they have gradually found their way down even to the kindergarten.

If children's celebrations were their own creations, the values celebrated would be ones that had been first of all understood and criticized. Even if these values were no more worthy than those foisted upon the children by adults, the immoral act of using ritual to enslave minds would not have been committed. The chances are, however, that the children, while using and drawing upon the good things in the culture, can improve upon what is handed them by their fathers. At least this will be so if the children come up through a schooling in which the creative social act is the central feature. For in that case the values they will choose to celebrate will in all likelihood be ones which promote the creative social act.

Voluntary cooperation, respect for personality, the sharing of experience, scientific method, and related values have a unique status among the possible ideal values that a child might celebrate. Of all values and value claims, these democratic-scientific procedural values alone can command loyalty without violence to the creative social act. They are procedures instrumental to the creative social act. Loyalty to them helps realize the act. In this they are in contrast to other procedural value claims, such as unrestricted competition, which destroy the creative social act. They are also in contrast to happiness as a value claim, because happiness has validity as a claim only so long as it does not conflict with the creative social act. Furthermore, happiness is essentially a product of the creative social act, while the democratic-scientific procedural values are instruments to the creative social act.

By encouraging the children to create their own forms, and by helping them choose wisely the objects to be celebrated, the school can turn the power of cultic symbolism to democratic ends. Ritualism and symbolism need no longer be the earmarks of enslaved or superstitious minds. They can instead be used to celebrate the very forces which challenge authoritarianism and ignorance.

CHAPTER XIV

Conclusion: Education for Religious Quality in Experience

The Nature of Religious Quality

The ultimate object of religious devotion is the creative social act. Broadly defined to include both the interactions of men with one another and the interactions of man and nature, the creative social act creates, tests, integrates, and differentiates value. It is the source of all good.

The creative social act has potentially the attributes of infinite goodness, power, and wisdom. Infinite goodness is the fact that the structure of value produced in the creative social act is infinitely reconstructible and forever continues to assimilate new values created in experience. Infinite power is the fact that in the creative social act powers are generated which transcend the sum total of energies contributed, and that all the energies of the universe—physical, social, and psychic—are potentially available to the creative act. Infinite wisdom is the fact that experience, wisdom's source, is never complete.

There are a number of modes of participation in the creative social act.

First, out of the participation of men with one another and with nature there emerge ideal values of existence to which the human participants dedicate the conduct of their lives. This is the valuational mode. Participative acts establish value claims tested in further acts which both integrate and differentiate value. Values are integrated when reflected-upon action reveals the cause-and-effect relations that exist between values as instrumental to one another. But the same acts which integrate values create new, unpredicted values. Differentiation is the seminal source upon which feeds the growing structure of integrated value.

The evolving structure of integrated value is an object of religious devotion. But it may not be taken at any given stage to be the final object of devotion. To pretend to have found, or to be misled into thinking one has found, the ultimate values of existence is the height of irreligion—a fact mythically expressed in the Christian doctrine of original sin. The ultimate object of devotion is not any given value or value structure, but that which produces all value—the creative social act.

Second, in the creative social act the individual finds an infinitely expansible community and an infinitely expansible self. This is the community mode. Voluntary cooperative participation creates both a community of experience and a community of aspiration. The participants develop characters disposed to find common interests with other members of the human race. Natural objects become involved in the social acts of men so that even nature acquires social meaning and becomes part of the community to which men feel they belong.

The quality and power of the community spirit pervade the individual participant and transform him as a personality. The variety of shared life is so extensive that the individual can find therein a role which defines his individuality. The community is the very source of his being insofar as it creates that which most distinguishes him as a man—his mentality. By helping to create a community he helps create a self, for he finds in the life of the community his life role, his mind, and the materials for building and enriching his personality.

Every man of integrity must develop a self of which he is unashamed and to which he is loyal. Every man of stability must find a community in which to realize his selfhood. But just as no finite value system may be taken as the ultimate object of religious devotion, neither may any finite community nor any finite self be so taken. Ethnocentrism and egocentrism go hand in hand. They are, after all, two forms of the same thing—a turning away from the creative social act in favor of a limited community or self, blind to the fact that thereby the source of both community and selfhood has been limited or destroyed. They are self-destructive—two forms of original sin leading only to death.

The paradox of loyalty to a given self and community with neither egocentrism nor ethnocentrism is resolvable only by placing ultimate loyalty in the creative social act. One must be true to one's self and one's community when integrity is at stake; yet renounce them to be born again when the creative social act is at stake.

Third, the ideal values which emerge from the social act mobilize for their realization the energies and resources of the participants, who dedicate their conduct to that end. This is the executive mode. Vitality and strength of character are the result of identification with an adequate and productive set of values. Identification is achieved when the use of intelligence reveals both the worth of values and actual ways of achieving them. Men do not have to be prodded, but are eager for action, when through the creative social act they achieve a vision of a more ideal existence, see actual ways to realize it, and are caught up in the spirit of a shared effort.

In order to be effective the dedicated group should work within and seek to preserve the community. But the group should refuse to acquiesce to whatever conduct of the community does violence to idealized values established through the use of shared intelligence. There is a place for both strongly aggressive and quietly acquiescent moods. A militant group intent upon the realization of ideals can make a daring and bold thrust. On the other hand, a group anxious to preserve the community may put emphasis upon tolerant acceptance of deficiencies; such a group wants to lead, but in a way that brings the community along.

But the militant group must be careful not to shatter the community in the violence of its attack; the withdrawn group must find the means for ultimate return with its contribution to the community; the accepting group must fight off the temptation to succumb to undesirable qualities pervading the life of the community. To shatter community, to succumb and lose creativity, to withdraw permanently, are destructive of the creative social act.

Fourth, the creative social act deeply involves the individual in a dramatic conflict between supporting and opposing forces, ending in consummation. The greater the range of value involved in the struggle and satisfied in the consummation, the more intensely religious is the quality of the experience in this, the aesthetic mode.

Fifth, the participants in the creative social act develop symbols and ceremonies which they use in the contemplative mood both to celebrate and to express the meaning of their shared life and common aspirations. This symbolism grows from the common life of the participants and serves to mobilize both their rational and nonrational energies in pursuit of their ideals. Worship serves not only to commemorate and vivify common ideals, but also to express their meaning. Symbolism brings the devotee face to face with the world of values to which logical discourse can only point.

Education as Cultivation of Religious Quality

The creative social act can and should be the characteristic feature of the school curriculum. It should be the basis of every school activity to which it is applicable, and should characterize the relations of pupils to one another, of pupils to teachers, of teachers to administrators, and of school to community. Young people can participate with one another and with their teachers in choosing, planning, and organizing their learning activities. Each activity can begin with a problem or enterprise agreed upon by the group (of which the teacher should be an integral part), according to criteria cooperatively determined. The members of the group can together formulate a plan for attacking the problem. Then, pooling their resources and organizing themselves in ways to promote the fullest contribution of every individual, they can cooperatively attack the problem, sharing their difficulties, experiences, findings, and successes at every possible point. The measure of the enterprise's success is the degree to which it ends with a feeling on the part of all, teacher and children alike, of significant individual and group accomplishment.

Through participation in the creative social act children and youth can experience, test, integrate, and differentiate value, so that there develops a growing structure of ideal value to which they can dedicate their lives. This process begins with the expression of mere likes and dislikes. But in the cooperative social situation these merely ejaculatory feelings come under the critical scrutiny of the participants, who test their worth and validity in the light of the way they work out when acted upon. Through such experiences of acting upon and critically evaluating desires, young people can transform them so that the relations of desires to one another and to the common welfare are revealed. The difference between ideal values of worth and validity, and mere childish whims, is the difference between desires that have not yet been tested and those that have been acted upon, reflected upon, and integrated with one another.

Acting upon their own desires and evaluating the outcomes are the primary experiences out of which children grow to valuational maturity. Yet this process would be too limited if it ignored the funded experience and judgment of the human race as to what is good and right. The findings of the race as to what is good should be made available to the children and seriously studied by them so that they can integrate such findings with their own. Yet the conclusions of the race should not be presented as more than value claims to be tested in the children's own experience. The first task of the school in respect to values is to develop the child's powers to make his own value judgments. If this task is taken seriously, there can be no ethical and axiological absolutes handed down to the child, but only claims presented to him for evaluation.

Young people can be helped to develop an expanding sense of community and selfhood through participation in the social act. Each individual can be helped to become a valued member of the group. As its solidarity increases, the group can be helped to identify itself with various elements of the community of which it is a part. In studying the life of the community, the group can have many opportunities for firsthand contact with and participation in that life. Through dramatization, role-playing, and other forms of vicarious experience, participation with the rest of the community can reach out to the whole world and back through all history.

Involvement in the social act enables the child or youth gradually to locate properly the ultimate sources of value, community and selfhood. His supreme loyalty should be to the social processes which create these. To foster this it is necessary that the school enable him to work and live accordingly. The work should be cooperative rather than individualistic and competitive, based on inquiry rather than on passive acceptance of authority. Through participation the individual can be helped to see that the promotion of the democratic process is more important than any particular outcome it may bring; that the preservation of the integrity of human relations is more important than any partial or limited goal upon which the participants may have their minds set; that methods of objective inquiry are more sacred than any belief, however cherished, those methods may threaten.

The child's successful response to the challenge of common problems in shared activity helps him develop executive quality in his conduct. The inquiries, problems, and projects chosen by his group should be of a kind to stimulate his powers and stretch his capacities. The child cannot and should not be protected from the difficulties, disappointments, and defeats inherent in his activities, but he can and should be protected from frustration. By experiencing difficult challenges ending in success, the child avoids the despair and cynicism which are the marks of irreligion, yet acquires the moral fiber and strength of character which enable him to meet life with courage and with faith in the potential transformability of existence for the better.

The child can be helped to develop and refine his natural tendency to commemorate and celebrate the ideal values revealed to him in the creative social act. Within their shared activities the children can create a symbolism which expresses for them better than can logical discourse the meaning of the ideals they are learning to cherish. Children can and should use disciplined methods of objective inquiry in pointing to and testing values. But the symbolic mode is needed to express the meaning of tested values, to keep them in the forefront of consciousness, and to mobilize nonrational as well as rational energies in their realization.

Involvement in the struggle between the forces supporting and opposing the social act gives the child's life dramatic quality, which terminates in aesthetic consummation when his activities come to a successful culmination. If his experiences have esthetic quality, they can bring him to grips with reality and confront him directly with the values of life. The cultivation of the arts of living is the school's greatest task. If it performs this function well, the school can help men create a new and better existence.

The foregoing principles point the way to animation of the entire curriculum by the several religious modes. They do not embody a new religion to be taught in the schools. Instead they state the conditions by which young people, their teachers, and others in the community are enabled to release the religious quality potential in their shared experience. Emergence in the common life of the people is the only way religion can develop in a democracy—in fact, this is the only way that religion in the real sense of the word can flourish at all. The common school, kept free of sectarian domination, is a proper institution for promoting that enterprise.

The participants in such an enterprise, teachers and students alike, would be embarked upon a new discovery. When individuals become involved in creative social activity, there is no knowing what will emerge. Undoubtedly many traditions will be cast aside and many established interests threatened. Yet the process is essentially constructive and conserving. The participants draw upon what is already established and stable in order to give their activities and inquiries a foundation, a perspective, materials to work with. The children in our schools are the inheritors of a varied and rich culture which exists by grace of the activities of others. The children's participation in the creative social act enables them to receive the heritage of ideal value which is rightfully theirs. But such participation also enables them to make their own maturing contributions to that heritage and rebuild it so that it can serve them better than it has ever served men before.

Bibliography

ABRAMS, RAY H., editor, "Organized Religion in the United States," *The Annals of the American Academy of Political and Social Science,* March, 1948.

ADLER, FELIX, *An Ethical Philosophy of Life*. New York: Appleton-Century-Crofts, Inc., 1918.

ALEXANDER, SAMUEL, *Space, Time and Deity*. London: Macmillan & Company, Ltd., 1920. 2 vols.

American Council on Education, Committee on Religion and Education, *The Relation of Religion to Public Education*. Washington, D. C.: The Council, 1947.

AMES, E. S., *Psychology of Religious Experience*. Boston: Houghton Mifflin Company, 1910.

——— *Religion*. New York: Henry Holt and Company, 1929.

BAILEY, A. E., *Art and Character*. New York: Abingdon Press, 1938.

BARNES, A. C. *The Art in Painting*. New York: Harcourt, Brace and Company, 1937.

BARON, SALO WITTMAYER, *Modern Nationalism and Religion*. New York: Harper & Brothers, 1947.

BENNETT, JOHN C., *Christian Ethics and Social Policy*. New York: Charles Scribner's Sons, 1946.

BEVAN, E. R., *Symbolism and Belief*. London: George Allen & Unwin, Ltd., 1938.

BOWER, W. C., *Church and State in Education*. Chicago: University of Chicago Press, 1944.

BRIDGMAN, P. W., *The Logic of Modern Physics*. New York: The Macmillan Company, 1927.

BRIGHTMAN, E. S., *A Philosophy of Religion*. New York: Prentice-Hall, Inc., 1946.

BRITTON, KARL, *"The Truth of Religious Propositions," Analysis*, October, 1935.

BRUBACHER, J. S., editor, *The Public Schools and Spiritual Values*. New York: Harper & Brothers, 1944.

BUERMEYER, L., *The Aesthetic Experience*. Merion, Pa.: The Barnes Foundation, 1924.

BURTT, EDWIN A., *Types of Religious Philosophy*. New York: Harper & Brothers, 1939.

CASE, S. J., *The Social Origins of Christianity*. Chicago: University of Chicago Press, 1927.

CASSIRER, ERNST, *An Essay on Man*. New Haven: Yale University Press, 1944.

——— *Language and Myth*. New York: Harper & Brothers, 1946.

——— *The Myth of the State*. New Haven: Yale University Press, 1946.

CHAVE, E. J., *A Functional Approach to Religious Education*. Chicago: University of Chicago Press, 1947.

COE, G. A., *The Psychology of Religion*. Chicago: University of Chicago Press, 1916.

COMTE, AUGUSTE, *The Positive Philosophy of Auguste Comte*. New York: W. Gowans, 1868.

DAVENPORT, F. M., *Primitive Traits in Religious Revivals*. New York: The Macmillan Company, 1905.

DEARMER, PERCY, *Art and Religion*. London: Student Christian Movement, 1924.

DELLA SETA, ALESSANDRO, *Religion and Art*. New York: Charles Scribner's Sons, 1914.

DEWEY, JOHN, *A Common Faith*. New Haven: Yale University Press, 1934.

——— *Art as Experience*. New York: Minton, Balch & Company, 1934.

——— *Democracy and Education*. New York: The Macmillan Company, 1916.

——— *Experience and Education*. New York: The Macmillan Company, 1938.

——— *Experience and Nature*. La Salle, Ill.: Open Court Publishing Company, 1929.

——— *Human Nature and Conduct*. New York: Random House, The Modern Library, 1930.

——— *Logic: The Theory of Inquiry*. New York: Henry Holt and Company, 1938.

——— *The Public and Its Problems*. New York: Henry Holt and Company, 1927.

——— *The Quest for Certainty*. London: George Allen & Unwin, Ltd., 1930.

——— *Theory of Valuation*. International Encyclopedia of Unified Science, Vol. 2, No. 4. Chicago: University of Chicago Press, 1939.

DEWEY, JOHN, and TUFTS, JAMES H., *Ethics*, revised edition. New York: Henry Holt and Company, 1932.

DIMOND, SYDNEY G., *Psychology of Methodist Revival*. London: Oxford University Press, 1926.

DIXON, W. M. *The Human Situation*. London: Edward Arnold & Company, 1937.

DUNLAP, KNIGHT, *Religion: Its Functions in Human Life*. New York: McGraw-Hill Book Company, Inc., 1946.

DURKHEIM, E., *The Elementary Forms of Religious Life*. London: George Allen & Unwin, Ltd., 1915.

ELLWOOD, CHARLES A., "The Social Function of Religion," *American Journal of Sociology*, November 1913.

FREUD, SIGMUND, "Totem and Taboo," A. A. Brill, editor, *The Basic Writings of Sigmund Freud*. New York: Random House, The Modern Library, 1938.

FRIESS, H. L., and SCHNEIDER, H. W., *Religion in Various Cultures*. New York: Henry Holt and Company, 1932.

GABRIEL, R. H., *The Course of American Democratic Thought*. New York: Ronald Press, 1944.

GREENE, T. H., *The Arts and the Art of Criticism*. Princeton: Princeton University Press, 1940.

HARRISON, JANE ELLEN, *Ancient Art and Ritual*. New York: Henry Holt and Company, 1913.

——— *Prolegomena to the Study of Greek Religion*, third edition. Cambridge: University Press, 1922.

——— *Themis: A Study of the Social Origins of Greek Religion*. Cambridge: Cambridge University Press, 1912.

HAYDEN, A. E., *Man's Search for the Good Life*. New York: Harper & Brothers, 1937.

——— *Quest of the Ages*, New York: The Philosophical Library, 1949.

HEILER, FREIDRICH, *Prayer, A Study in the History and Psychology of Religion*. New York: Oxford University Press, 1932.

HERTZ, RICHARD, *Chance and Symbol*. Chicago: University of Chicago Press, 1948.

HOCKING, W. E., *Living Religious and a World Faith*. New York: The Macmillan Company, 1940.

HÖFFDING, HARALD, *The Philosophy of Religion*, second edition. New York: The Macmillan Company, 1914.

HYMA, ALBERT, *Christianity, Capitalism and Communism*. Ann Arbor, Mich.: G. Wahr, 1937.

JAMES, E. O., *The Social Function of Religion.* Nashville: Cokesbury Press, no date.

JAMES, WILLIAM, *The Varieties of Religious Experience.* New York: Random House, Modern Library Edition.

JOHNSON, F., ERNEST, *The Church and Society.* New York: Abingdon-Cokebury Press, 1935.

JONES, RUFUS M., *Mysticism and Democracy in the English Commonwealth.* Cambridge, Mass: Harvard University Press, 1932.

JUNG, C. G., *Modern Man in Search of a Soul.* London: K. Paul, Trench, Trubner & Company, 1933.

——— *Psychology and Religion.* New Haven: Yale University Press, 1938.

KANT, I., *Religion Within the Limits of Reason Alone.* Chicago: Open Court Publishing Company, 1934.

KELLEY, EARL C., *Education for What Is Real.* New York: Harper & Brothers, 1947.

KING, IRVING, *The Development of Religion.* New York: The Macmillan Company, 1910.

KLUCKHOHN, CLYDE, "Myths and Rituals: A General Theory," *Harvard Theological Review*, January, 1942.

LANGER, SUSANNE K., *Philosophy in a New Key.* New York: Penguin Books, Inc., 1948.

LEEUW, G. VAN DER, *Religion in Essence and Manifestation.* London, George Allen & Unwin, 1938.

LEUBA, JAMES H., *A Psychological Study of Religion.* New York: The Macmillan Company, 1912.

——— *Psychology of Religious Mysticism.* New York: Harcourt, Brace and Company, 1925.

MACMURRAY, JOHN, *The Structure of Religious Experience.* New Haven: Yale University Press, 1936.

MALINOWSKY, B., *Magic, Science and Religion.* Glencoe, Ill.: The Free Press, 1948.

MANNHEIM, KARL, *Ideology and Utopia.* London: K. Paul, Trench, Trubner & Company, 1936.

MARETT, R. R., *Sacraments of Simple Folks.* Oxford: Clarendon Press, 1938.

——— *The Threshold of Religion*, second edition. London: Methuen & Co., Ltd., 1914.

MEAD, G. H. *Mind, Self and Society.* Chicago: University of Chicago Press, 1938.

MEAD, G. H., *Philosophy of the Act*. Chicago: University of Chiago Press, 1938.

——— *Philosophy of the Present*. Chicago: Open Court Publishing Company, 1932.

MILLER, HUGH, *The Community of Man*. New York: The Macmillan Company, 1949.

MOEHLMAN, C. H., *School and Church: The American Way*. New York: Harper & Brothers, 1944.

MOORE, G. F., *History of Religions*. New York: Charles Scribner's Sons, 1937. 2 vols.

——— *The Birth and Growth of Religion*. New York: Charles Scribner's Sons, 1923.

MORRIS, C. W., *Signs, Language and Behavior*. New York: Prentice-Hall, Inc., 1946.

National Education Association, Department of Elementary School Principals, Twenty-sixth Yearbook. *Spiritual Values in the Elementary School*. Washington, D. C.: The Association, 1947.

NIEBUHR, H. RICHARD, *The Social Sources of Denominationalism*. New York: Henry Holt and Company, 1929.

NIEBUHR, REINHOLD, *The Nature and Destiny of Man*. New York: Charles Scribner's Sons, 1941-1943. 2 vols.

NORTHROP, F. S. C., *The Meeting of East and West*. New York: The Macmillan Company, 1946.

PERRY, RALPH BARTON, *Puritanism and Democracy*. New York: The Vanguard Press, 1944.

POPE, LISTON, *Millhands and Preachers*. New Haven: Yale University Press, 1942.

PRATT, J. B., *The Religious Consciousness*. New York: The Macmillan Company, 1923.

RAUP, R. B., BENNE, K. D., AXTELLE, G. E., and SMITH, B. O., "The Discipline of Practical Judgment in a Democratic Society," *Twenty-eighth Yearbook of the National Society of College Teachers of Education*. Chicago: University of Chicago Press, 1942.

RAUSCHENBUSH, WALTER, *Christianity and the Social Crisis*. New York: The Macmillan Company, 1909.

ROYCE, JOSIAH, *The Problem of Christianity*. New York: The Macmillan Company, 1913. 2 vols.

SANTAYANA, GEORGE, *Reason in Religion*, second edition. New York: Charles Scribner's Sons, 1933.

SCHMIDT, WILHELM, *The Origin and Growth of Religion: Facts and Theories*. New York: The Dial Press, 1935.

SCHWEITZER, ALBERT, *The Philosophy of Civilization*. New York: The Macmillan Company, 1949.

SELLERS, R. W., *Religion Coming of Age*. New York: The Macmillan Company, 1931.

SIMKHOVITCH, VLADIMIR G., *Toward the Understanding of Jesus*. New York: The Macmillan Company, 1947.

SMITH, T. V., "The Religious Bearings of a Secular Mind: George Herbert Mead," *Journal of Religion*, April, 1932.

SMITH, W. ROBERTSON, *The Religion of the Semites*, third edition. London: A. and C. Black, Ltd., 1923.

STARBUCK, E. D., *The Psychology of Religion*, third edition. New York: Charles Scribner's Sons, 1912.

TAWNEY, R. H., *Religion and the Rise of Capitalism*. New York: Penguin Books, Inc., 1947.

THAYER, V. T., *Religion in Public Education*. New York: The Viking Press, 1947.

THOULESS, R. H., *An Introduction to the Psychology of Religion*, second edition. New York: The Macmillan Company, 1936.

TILLICH, PAUL, *The Protestant Era*. Chicago: University of Chicago Press, 1948.

——— "The Religious Symbol," *Journal of Liberal Religion*, Summer, 1940.

TOY, C. H., *Introduction to History of Religions*. Boston: Ginn & Company, 1913.

TOYNBEE, A. J., *A Study of History*, abridged edition. New York: Oxford University Press, 1947.

——— *Christianity and Civilization*. Wallingford, Pa.: Pendle Hill, 1948.

TROELTSCH, E., *The Social Teaching of the Christian Churches*. New York: The Macmillan Company, 1931. 2 vols.

UNDERHILL, EVELYN, *Worship*. New York: Harper & Brothers, 1937.

URBAN, W. M., *Language and Reality*. London: George Allen & Unwin, 1939.

——— "Symbolism as a Theological Principle," *Journal of Religion*, January, 1939.

UREN, A. P., *Recent Religious Psychology*. Edinburgh: T. and T. Clark, 1928.

VOGT, VON OGDEN, *Art and Religion*. New Haven: Yale University Press, 1921.

WACH, J., *Sociology of Religion*. Chicago: University of Chicago Press, 1944.

WEBER, MAX, *The Protestant Ethic and the Spirit of Capitalism*. New York: Charles Scribner's Sons, 1930.

WHITE, LANCELOT L., *The Next Development in Man*. New York: Henry Holt and Company, 1948.

WHITEHEAD, A. N., *Religion in the Making*. New York: The Macmillan Company, 1926.

WIEMAN, HENRY N., *Methods of Private Religious Living*. New York: The Macmillan Company, 1929.

——— *Normative Psychology of Religion*. New York: Thomas Y. Crowell Company, 1935.

——— *Religious Experience and Scientific Method*. New York: The Macmillan Company, 1928.

——— *The Source of Human Good*. Chicago: University of Chicago Press, 1945.

——— and MELAND, B. E., *American Philosophies of Religion*. New York: Willett, Clark and Company, 1936.

——— and NORTON, WALTER M., *The Growth of Religion*. Chicago: Willett, Clark and Company, 1938.

WILLIAMS, JOHN PAUL, *The New Education and Religion*. New York: Association Press, 1945.

WOODBURN, ANGUS S., *The Religious Attitude*. New York: The Macmillan Company, 1927.

Index